The Hidden Epidemic

An examination of suicide in the UK

TIM WATKINS
for
LIFE SURFING

Life Surfing
Box 124, R&R Consulting Centre
41 St. Isan Road
Heath
Cardiff CF14 4LW

ISBN-13: 978-1492772361
ISBN-10: 1492772364

ABOUT THE AUTHOR

Tim Watkins is a Wellbeing Coach, Trainer and founder-director of Life Surfing, a not-for-profit company established to help prevent mental illness and to promote wellbeing.

Tim Watkins graduated from the University of Wales College Cardiff with a first class honours degree in 1990.

Between 1990 and 1997 he worked as a research officer for the Welsh Consumer Council where he researched and wrote a range of reports including *In Deep Water* an investigation into problems in the aftermath of the North Wales ("Towyn") floods of 1990, and *Quality of Life and Quality of Service* an investigation into the promotion of quality of life in residential homes for older people.

Following a severe and enduring episode of depression that lasted through 1997 to 2000, Tim Watkins began volunteering and later working for the charity Depression Alliance, running its Wales office, and steering it to becoming an independent charity in its own right in 2005. He continued to run the charity until 2010.

Between 2001 and 2010, the Welsh Government appointed him to sit on the *Health & Wellbeing Council for Wales* and the *Burrows-Greenwell Review of Mental Health in Wales.* He also played a key role in developing the *Healthy Minds at Work* project, during which he wrote *Taking Control*, an audio self-help book for people affected by depression, and oversaw the development of the award-winning *Depression Busting* self-management programme for people affected by depression.

In October 2010, along with Julia Kaye and Paul Clarke, Tim Watkins formed Life Surfing in order to address public wellbeing in people experiencing stress or whose life circumstances put them at risk of developing mental illness and people experiencing mild/moderate common mental illnesses such as anxiety and depression.

In addition to writing the growing range of Life Surfing publications, Tim Watkins, with Julia Kaye, has co-authored a range of training workshops:

- o *How to Help in a Crisis*: a one-day workshop for people who want to learn how to help and support people with mental health problems

- o *Distress to De-stress*: a 2 hour workshop for people who want to learn how to manage stress

- o *Getting to Sleep*: a 2 hour workshop for people experiencing stress-related sleep problems

- o *Banish your Blues*: a one-day workshop for people who want to learn how to self-manage depression

Tim Watkins provides one-to-one Wellbeing Coaching sessions to anyone that wants to improve their personal wellbeing either face-to-face at our consulting rooms in Cardiff or via Skype (please visit our website – www.life-surfing.com – for further information)

Foreword

Hardly a week goes by without a suicide making the headlines. Some cases are truly appalling:

- ❑ The South Wales father who battered his wife and four children to death before hanging himself
- ❑ The Yorkshire mother who took her daughter for a walk up to the disused viaduct, held her hand, then jumped
- ❑ The London man who set fire to his car while he and his children sat in the back
- ❑ The North Wales man who gassed himself and his children by running a petrol lawn mower in the back of his car.

Less prominent, but in their own way equally tragic, are the daily cases of people who slip away unseen, no longer able to cope with the world, taking their own lives.

That we should do something to prevent such events is without question. Problems arise when we try to agree on what we should do. What should a suicide prevention strategy look like?

After several decades of failed suicide prevention strategies based around removing the means of suicide while doing little to remove the motivation, one is tempted to go further than simply saying that these initiatives have failed. One is tempted to say that a very narrow medical model, with a focus on individual pathology, actually adds to the number of UK suicides.

This report draws upon witness testimony as well as published statistical and secondary data to show why, despite successive suicide reduction initiatives, the suicide rate remains stubbornly high.

This report compels those with an interest in suicide reduction to think about tackling the social causes of suicide rather than stigmatising and pathologising those who are driven to suicide.

Tim Watkins

CONTENTS

Author's Note

This report was originally written in the summer of 2003, following an analysis of a survey conducted for a London-based mental health charity.

Although more recent statistics may now be available, many of the points made in this report are if anything even more relevant to the post-credit crunch world than was the case at the time. Indeed, many of the trends toward fragmented communities, isolated individuals and an end to traditional patterns of employment and housing have accelerated since 2008.

Most chillingly, the increases in suicides predicted in the report – particularly those in men have come true with a vengeance. Statistics released by the Office for National Statistics for 2010-11 show an alarming 30% increase in male suicides. These come despite the implementation of new suicide reduction strategies, and fly in the face of claims that restrictions on the sale of paracetamol caused reductions in the suicide rate in the mid-2000s.

In 2003, the report claimed that reductions in suicide were much more likely to be the result of improvements in the economy. However, the report showed that these improvements were precarious. Our current economic difficulties have exposed the many social and economic problems highlighted here a decade ago.

For these reasons, I believe that there is still much to be gained from reading this work and from encouraging further debate about the way we respond to suicide and its causes.

Tim Watkins, June 2013.

Tim Watkins

Executive Summary

Introduction

There is a creeping epidemic in the UK. It is an epidemic that now accounts for most deaths in young people. It is an epidemic that takes parents away from children. Every 80 minutes, a life is lost to it. Every day two children will die from it. Every year it results over 6,000 deaths and between 150,000 and 200,000 hospital admissions. It is an epidemic that we fear even discussing. It is suicide.

Since 1970, successive governments have attempted to develop suicide reduction policies, only to see the suicide rate rise remorselessly.

One reason why the epidemic has grown is that we tend to dismiss it as something that happens to other people, elsewhere. It is not. The precipitating factors in suicides and suicide attempts are life events such as:

- o Redundancy or the threat of redundancy
- o Bereavement
- o Unemployment
- o Workplace stress
- o Bullying
- o Separation/divorce
- o Housing problems
- o Debt
- o Prolonged ill health.

These are factors that all of us experience at one time or another. They are factors that can create levels of stress that alter brain chemistry and thought patterns in ways that impair rational thinking. For many people (between 10 and 14 percent at present, 20-25 percent at some time in their lives) the result is a period of depressive illness. For a sizeable number it will result in serious self-harm and/or attempted suicide. For some it will result in death by suicide.

Rational Suicide?

There are many public, and often controversial suicides: war criminals ending their lives to cheat the hangman, people with terminal illnesses wishing to regain control and/or end their pain, businessmen who leap from their office buildings when the stock market crashes.

A number of commentators have raised the possibility that some of these suicides may be rational. A soldier diving on a grenade to prevent the rest of his unit being killed commits a rational suicide. Oates stepping out into the Antarctic night committed a rational suicide. To take one's life because one has lost a business, a job, a family or a fortune, is irrational. Life goes on. People who lose businesses build new ones. People who lose jobs get new ones. People who divorce, re-marry. Even defeated generals and bankrupted stockbrokers rebuild their lives.

The life events associated with suicide are those that lead to depression. It is the irrational thinking that is a symptom of depression that makes suicide seem rational to those contemplating it.

At least 75 percent of people who take their own lives had depression at the time of their death. It is reasonable to suspect that many of the remaining 25 percent had some degree of undiagnosed depression prior to their deaths.

When reasoning is impaired by depression, suicide can appear to be a reasonable course of action. It is not that major life events are that bad, it is just that those affected believe them to be.

Who commits suicide – and why?

Suicide statistics are important because they give an indication of how many people commit suicide. Moreover, since the same agencies gather suicide statistics in the same way, day-in/day-out, they provide a picture of how the numbers committing suicide change over time.

Statisticians can give an indication of which groups of people are "at risk" of committing suicide by examining sociological factors such as: occupation, age, sex, marital status and education.

Three-quarters of suicide attempts are by women. However, two-thirds of successful suicides are by men. This is largely explained by the chosen methods. Women tend to choose "passive" methods, such as drug overdoses, which allow the possibility of rescue. Men tend to opt for "active" methods, such as jumping from high buildings, which allow little possibility of rescue.

In the 1970s, the older you were, the more likely you were to take your own life. This has dramatically reversed in the ensuing 30 years. Men aged 25-44 are the most likely to take their own lives. However, the biggest increase has been in young men aged 16-24. The rate of suicide in women aged 16-24 (although much lower) has also risen sharply in recent years.

These are the only significant personal predictors of risk. There are, however, social circumstances that can dramatically affect the risk of suicide. Social isolation is the biggest predictor. People who live alone, or people who live with strangers are at the highest risk. This is especially so if they lack social networks.

Life stressors play an important role. Bereavement is the life stressor most associated with suicide. However, unemployment, homelessness, relationship breakdown and debt are also important factors.

Nevertheless, not everyone who has these characteristics and stresses will take their own lives. Furthermore, many suicides are by people who do not have any of the expected risk criteria. This raises questions about how an official suicide reduction policy should operate.

How to respond to suicide

Successive governments since the 1970s have set suicide reduction targets that have failed to deliver a reduction in the suicide rate. Although short term targets (such as cutting suicide in old people and cutting paracetomol self-poisonings) have been temporarily realised, the UK suicide rate has remained stubbornly high. Much of the failure is explained by the way suicide prevention has operated.

Detaining people at risk of suicide

For the most part, suicide has been dealt with within the framework of legislation that allows for the compulsory detention and treatment of those considered to be at risk of harming themselves and/or others.

This legislation has been used to remove people at risk of suicide from the means, and/or to remove the means of suicide from individuals thought to be at risk. While this approach may be effective in individual cases, it has failed as a social policy.

We now incarcerate more people in mental hospitals and units than ever before. Since 1990 there has been a 50% increase in UK detentions under the Mental Health Act. In Wales, there has been a 100% increase in detentions. However, the suicide rate has seen only a tiny fall which is more likely explained by the prosperity of the late 1990s and early 2000s than by locking people up.

The inability to predict risk is a particular problem. Eighty-five percent of people known to have mental health problems who take their lives are dismissed as being no-risk or low-risk by medical practitioners – 45% in the week before their deaths! Furthermore, the prospect of detention and compulsory treatment under the Mental Health Act serves to deter many people from seeking professional help for problems which eventually result in suicide.

The real problem isn't that the majority of suicidal individuals evade treatment. On the contrary, a historical shortage of resources mean that mental health services routinely fail to treat people who are at risk. The problem is that people with mild-moderate depression are deterred from seeking help at a time when their illness could be easily treated, only to turn up at a later stage with severe illness or as a suicide statistic.

Of course, where an individual is clearly at risk, it is necessary to treat him or her. However, speculative detention is counter-productive because of its deterrent effect on people whose illness could otherwise be treated before it becomes life threatening.

Removing the means of suicide

Removing or restricting the means of suicide from society may also be of value. The two biggest falls in the suicide rate in the 20th century were the result of the introduction of natural gas in the 1970s, and the introduction of catalytic converters in the 1990s. However, these reductions were temporary. Once the changes become widely known, people simply opted for alternative methods. Similarly, the recent restriction on the sale of Paracetomol has resulted in a decrease in the use of this substance in self-poisoning. However, the success has been overstated, as the number of self-hangings has risen proportionately. Hanging is the suicide method of choice in the majority of cases, and one cannot see a reasonable way of restricting the sale of rope, string, electrical cable, telephone wire, etc.

Once again, if it is possible to restrict the means of suicide, this should be done. For example, we should restrict the use of the antidepressants Amitriptyline and Dothiepin because they account for over half of all antidepressant self-poisonings. With 28 alternatives available, it seems an unnecessary risk to give toxic medication to people affected by depression.

We also need more research into the claim that newer SSRI antidepressants cause some people to become suicidal. Since these are the only alternative to earlier and much more toxic tricyclic antidepressants, we need to understand the relative risks of both, and of doing nothing.

Unfortunately, restricting access to the means of suicide can only be part of an overall strategy. Often restriction is more a test of human ingenuity – in the end, when the desire is strong enough, the means will be found.

Removing the desire for suicide

There is, then, no quick fix to suicide. We cannot predict risk, and allowing people to be detained and treated against their will simply deters people from seeking help. Furthermore, if all those potentially at risk of suicide were to come forward, most would have to be turned away by our over-stretched mental health services.

Nor does restricting the means of suicide offer much prospect of cutting the suicide rate. We cannot take the all potential means of suicide out of society. Many people take their lives using ordinary household items. This leads us to the only real solution – to address the desire for suicide.

In 1888, Emile Durkheim, one of the founders of modern social science, argued that the overall rate of suicide was a measure of the cohesion and mental wellbeing of a whole society. All else being equal, a rise in the rate of suicide indicated lower cohesion and less wellbeing.

The additional cohesiveness of a nation at war was demonstrated twice in the twentieth century. The 1914-1918 war saw the lowest UK suicide rate in a century. The 1939-1945 war saw a low, although slightly higher suicide rate. The period of social and economic upheaval between 1974 and 1996 saw the longest continual rise in the suicide rate.

Contemporary UK society is dangerously stressed and dangerously fragmented. Living in a global economy has increased the stresses faced by individuals to danger levels. In the UK we work longer (but not smarter) and for less than our EU competitors. Nevertheless, our productivity remains 20% lower than the EU. Our housing market is out of control – only 10% of our housing is not owner-occupied, forcing people on low incomes into private housing that they cannot afford. Debt levels in the UK are high and rising. Meanwhile the job market remains unstable, with few employees able to count on their employment lasting beyond three years.

With so many stresses, people need wide social networks to help them cope. However, UK society has never been more fragmented. Families are more isolated than ever before, with distortions in the housing market making even community-wide extended families impossible to maintain. Home-centred activities (television, DVDs, CDs, computer games) have become the preferred forms of recreation in most households. The one popular outside activity – cinema – is a particularly unsocial one. Neighbourliness is in decline. Less than half of people under 30 are on speaking terms with their next door neighbours.

The high UK rate of suicide is a warning. We can choose to go on as we have been doing, and risk an even higher suicide rate. Alternatively, we can begin to take steps to create a healthier society with lower suicide rates for the future.

With the prosperity of the late 1990s and early 200s at an end, we can expect the suicide rate to begin rising again into the foreseeable future. However, we can begin to address the desire for suicide.

Tim Watkins

Introduction

There is a creeping epidemic in the UK. It is an epidemic that now accounts for most deaths in young people. It is an epidemic that takes parents away from children. Every 80 minutes, a life is lost to it. Every day two children will die from it. Every year it results over 6,000 deaths and between 150,000 and 200,000 hospital admissions. This year, twice as many people will die from it as will die in road traffic accidents. It is an epidemic that we fear even discussing. It is suicide.

Since 1970, successive governments have attempted to develop suicide reduction policies, only to see the suicide rate rise remorselessly. Policies targeting particular groups such as the elderly or young men often result in a temporary fall in the rate for that group, but with a proportionate rise in the rate for other groups. Similarly, the most recent suicide policies have resulted in a fall in the suicide rate in the southeast of England (outside London) but with a remorseless rise in Scotland, Wales and the north of England.

One reason why the epidemic has grown is that we tend to dismiss it as something that happens to other people, elsewhere. It is not. The precipitating factors in suicides and suicide attempts are life events such as:

o   Redundancy
o   Bereavement
o   Workplace stress
o   Bullying
o   Separation/divorce
o   Housing problems
o   Debt
o   Prolonged ill health
o   Mental illness.

At least some of these are factors that we all experience at one time or another. They are factors that can create levels of stress that alter biological and psychological process in ways that impair rational thinking. For many people (between 10 and 14 percent at present, 20-25 percent at some time in their lives) the result is a period of depressive illness. For a sizeable number (150,000 to 200,000 per year) it will result in serious self-harm and/or attempted suicide. For some (over 6,000 per year) it will result in death by suicide.

It is widely held that some people are predisposed to depression and suicide. Whether this is due to genes, childhood trauma, mother/child bonding, etc has yet to be established, and research continues in all of these areas. However, a person does not have to be predisposed to suicide; under the right conditions and faced with enough stress, anyone can become suicidal.

The treatment of the depression that underpins more than 75 percent of all suicides is the subject of ongoing discussion and debate. Where depression is severe, the best available evidence is that a combination of medication and "talking treatments" produces the best result. In mild or moderate depression the effect of medication tends to be smaller, while talking treatments such as Cognitive Behavioural Therapy (CBT) have proved especially effective.

Unfortunately, talking treatments are not widely available. Most people affected by depression will receive medication alone. Since this is not as effective, it may prolong illness unnecessarily. Furthermore, medication still carries an association with the "happy pill" culture of the 1960s. This creates fears about side effects and dependency that can cause people to avoid seeking medical help.

Mental health legislation allowing for detention and compulsory treatment of people affected by mental illness also helps deter people from seeking help. In the last decade there has been a 50 percent increase in the number of people compulsorily detained under mental health law in response to growing fears about the risks posed by people with mental illness to themselves and/or others.

This state-sponsored discrimination can deter people from seeking help when they first develop the symptoms of mental ill-health. Around half of all people with depression at any one time do not seek formal help. Some may fall back on the support of family and friends, and this may help them through their illness. Many will not, and will turn up at a later stage with more severe depression. Some may take their lives without ever asking for formal help.

This large pool of undiagnosed people who actively avoid formal services because of the discrimination surrounding mental illness poses a massive problem to those drawing up suicide reduction strategies. This is because most strategies have focused on either taking people away from the means of killing themselves and/or removing the means from people.

Removing the means but not the desire is problematic. While lack of means may prevent an "impulse suicide attempt", it may also simply test human ingenuity in finding means that the authorities have not foreseen. While people may not, for example, have Paracetamol at home, they will have bleach, rope, shoe laces, kitchen knives, etc.

This report challenges the belief that focusing on individuals (especially if the main approach is to remove the means but not the desire) will reduce the rate of suicide. The report will show that wider societal factors must be taken into account.

Some recognition of this appears with the publication of the *National Suicide Prevention Strategy for England* (Department of Health 2002):

"The factors associated with suicide are many and varied – they include social circumstances, biological vulnerability, mental ill-health, life events and access to means. A coherent, co-ordinated suicide prevention strategy therefore needs the collaboration of a wide range of organisations and individuals". (p3)

This report sets out the case for a new approach to suicide reduction based on an attack on the social factors that precipitate suicides and suicide attempts, together with a much greater focus on mental health promotion. In part, this is in agreement with the new *National Suicide Prevention Strategy for England*, but in part it argues that we must go further.

Methods

This report is partly the outcome of a survey of people who had attempted suicide. The survey was conducted in March 2001, and resulted in valuable qualitative evidence about how people felt in the period immediately prior to their attempted suicide. This is unusual data, and goes a long way toward humanising suicide.

The report also draws upon quantitative data from the survey and secondary data from government and academic sources to examine the prevalence of suicide and attempted suicide together with the factors that underlie them. Drawing on the evidence, this report will go on to examine the way the state, through mental health services, has tried to deal with the suicide epidemic.

In the last chapter of the report, we look at what could be done to promote mental health as a means of reducing the rate of suicide. This is based on the view that the rate of suicide in any particular country is a measure of the general mental health of the overall society. If this is so, then it will require improvements in the mental health of the whole society to bring about significant falls in the rate of suicide.

The purpose of this report is to raise awareness of suicide, to prompt debate about our response to it.

Rational Suicide or Irrational Thinking?

Suicide is a real option, a way out when you get to the stage you need a way out. I really don't think that unless you have suffered – I mean really suffered – from depression, you can tell somebody who wants to commit suicide that it is not the thing to do... If you have suffered from depression for many years, and there is little hope of respite, I think you should be allowed to take your own life and not be a burden on your family. – Survey respondent.

There are many public examples of suicide. Stockbrokers leaping from skyscrapers during the Wall Street crash of 1929, and Axis leaders and generals killing themselves rather than face defeat in 1945 are some of the more famous. Since apparently rational people – often those who have scaled the heights of their chosen professions – choose suicide as a means of dealing with apparently insurmountable problems, maybe suicide is itself a rational act.

However, few suicides take place in such extreme circumstances. Most involve some degree of mental impairment and incapacity. More often, suicide really is "a permanent solution to a temporary problem".

Rational suicide?

Suicide can be rational, but very rarely, and mostly in extreme living conditions. In war, for example, soldiers have dived on top of grenades, so that the loss of a single soldier saves a whole unit. Similarly, captured spies and partisans, knowing they were doomed, found ways to take their own lives rather than risk giving away their networks. Another extreme example of altruistic suicide is that of Oates stepping out into the Antarctic night toward the end of Scott's doomed Antarctic expedition. In these circumstances, the individual dies to save the lives of others. This would seem to be both rational and moral.

More questionable are those instances where death is inevitable, and suicide becomes a means of "re-empowering" the doomed individual.

Thus war criminals may choose suicide rather than face capture. Similarly, those guilty of capital crimes may opt to shoot it out with the police rather than spend years on death row prior to being killed at the state's pleasure.

These instances often appear morally dubious. There is an element of cowardice involved in criminals' decisions to take their own lives rather than face the consequences of their actions. However, there is also rationality in cheating the hangman.

Re-empowerment also seems to be a key element in voluntary euthanasia. In addition to providing a permanent form of pain relief, euthanasia would seem to return an element of control over life that illness had taken away. This may be as true in cases of prolonged mental anguish as it is for physical pain.

Fortunately, these forms of suicide are the extreme. Most people choose to end their lives for altogether less rational reasons. To take one's life because one has lost a business, a job, a family or a fortune, is irrational. Life goes on. People who lose businesses build new ones. People who lose jobs get new ones. People who divorce, re-marry. Even defeated generals and bankrupted stockbrokers rebuild their lives.

This is not to belittle the trauma experienced by people going through these events. It is only to point out that such life events are seldom as dark as they seem to those inside the experience of them. Time really is a great healer.

Depression and irrational thinking

The life events often associated with suicide are those associated with depression. Indeed, one might argue that depression is a common symptom of extreme events.

Around three quarters of suicides are by people affected by depression (Department of Health 2001). One can reasonably suspect that many of the others are due to undiagnosed mental health problems by people not in touch with formal mental health services.

Depression is most commonly thought of as affecting mood. However, those affected by depression often point to the physical symptoms of the illness as being the most troubling. These include aches and pains, disorders of the digestive system, headaches and sleep disorders. They may also include problems with the functioning of the brain, such as memory loss, loss of concentration, impaired motor skills and – most important when examining suicide – *impaired reasoning.*

Being irrational, then, can be a symptom of depression. Furthermore, the effect of irrational thinking is often to dampen brain functioning to an even greater degree. People affected by depression may become locked into a downward spiral of (among other symptoms) irrational thinking undermining brain functioning and impaired brain functioning undermining rational thought.

It is an understanding of this process that has informed the development of the relatively successful Cognitive Behavioural Therapy (CBT), which intervenes in the patient's thought process in an attempt to reverse the process into a virtuous spiral in which rational thought enhances brain functioning.

David D. Burns (1990) identifies ten forms of distorted thinking common to those affected by depression, where intervention can help overcome depression:

> **All or nothing thinking**: "You see things in black or white categories. If a situation falls short of perfect, you see it as a total failure."
>
> **Overgeneralisation**: "You see a single negative event, such as a romantic rejection or a career reversal, as a never-ending pattern of defeat by using words such as 'always' or 'never' when you think about it."
>
> **Mental filtering**: "you pick out a single negative detail and dwell on it exclusively, so that your vision of all reality becomes darkened…"
>
> **Discounting the positive**: "You reject positive experiences by insisting they 'don't count'. If you do a good job, you may tell yourself it wasn't good enough or that anyone could have

done as well. Discounting the positive takes the joy out of life and makes you feel inadequate and unrewarded."

Jumping to conclusions: "You interpret things negatively when there are no facts to support your conclusions – *Mind Reading*: Without checking it out, you arbitrarily conclude someone is reacting negatively to you – *Fortune telling*: You predict that things will turn out badly."

Magnification: "You exaggerate the importance of your problems and shortcomings, or you minimise the importance of your desirable qualities."

Emotional Reasoning: "You assume that your negative emotions necessarily reflect the way things really are: 'I feel terrified about going on aeroplanes – it must be dangerous to fly'."

Should statements: "You tell yourself that things *should* be the way you hoped or expected them to be… 'Musts', 'oughts' and 'have-tos' are similar offenders. *Should* statements that are directed against yourself lead to guilt and frustration. *Should* statements that are directed against other people or the world in general lead to anger and frustration."

Labelling: "Labelling is an extreme form of all-or-nothing thinking… Labelling is quite irrational because you are not the same as what you do. Human beings exist, but 'fools', 'losers' and 'jerks' do not. These labels are just useless abstractions that lead to anger, anxiety, frustration and low self-esteem."

Personalisation and blame: "Personalization occurs when you hold yourself personally responsible for an event that isn't entirely under your control... Personalization leads to guilt, shame, and feelings of inadequacy." (pp40-41)

Most people are able to dismiss distorted thoughts for what they are. For someone affected by depression, this is not so easy – if your mind isn't working, what will you use to determine the validity of thoughts? A malfunctioning mind allows irrational thoughts to appear realistic. Moreover, for those with depression, the persistence of such thoughts is severe. It can be like a voice in your head, constantly highlighting your inadequacies and blaming you for all of life's ills.

Understanding this, one can glimpse how, at its most severe, distorted thinking might make suicide *seem* rational. As one of our respondents pointed out:

> *It is easy to blame external factors in any suicide attempt. But what essentially pushes you to it is the sense of total despair and hopelessness which sometimes has little to do with your 'objective' circumstances and all with very little self-worth. It makes you feel that everybody – your family, friends, even your children – the whole world would be better off without you.*

Suicidal thoughts

Thoughts about death and suicide are, perhaps surprisingly, common in the population at large. Among those affected by depression, however, these thoughts may be more persistent. Furthermore, because of the way depression distorts rational thought, these thoughts may appear to be more reasonable. Nevertheless, it is only a minority of those affected by depression who act on suicidal thoughts.

When someone is affected by depression, things seem darker than they are. The end of a marriage or the end of a particular job may, at the time, appear to be the end of life itself. Faced with feelings of overwhelming hopelessness and helplessness, a person so affected may believe suicide is a rational and reasonable course of action.

At the point when suicidal thoughts become persistent and realistic (as opposed to fleeting and unreasonable), the affected individual is in real danger.

Permanent solutions to temporary problems

To understand why apparently rational people take their own lives, one has to understand what happens to people's critical faculties when the areas of the brain that house them become depressed.

Major life events, mainly – though not exclusively – negative, can result in depression. Depression results in impaired reasoning of the kind outlined above:

- o   All or nothing thinking
- o   Over-generalisation
- o   Mental filtering
- o   Discounting the positive
- o   Jumping to conclusions
- o   Magnification
- o   Emotional reasoning
- o   Should statements
- o   Labelling
- o   Personalisation and blame.

When reasoning is impaired in this way, suicide can appear to be a reasonable course of action. It is not that major life events *are* that bad, it is just that those affected *believe* them to be.

In addition to believing that things are really bad, people who go on to attempt suicide or to take their lives are often haunted by a belief in the hopelessness of their situation and their potential future together with a feeling of their own helplessness. Such feelings may be compounded by extreme feelings of guilt that result in their feeling that the world would be better off without them.

With around one person an hour in the UK taking their own lives (two teenagers every day), the problem facing us would seem to be of identifying which individuals are at risk, and of getting to them and treating them before they take their lives.

Chapter two will look at the statistical information currently available on suicides. It will ask whether it is possible to identify those individuals at risk and to intervene in ways that prevent suicide.

Who commits suicide – and why?

"If you are choking to death in a restaurant you have a better chance of survival than if you tell your best friend you are thinking of killing yourself" – B. Kopans

Suicide statistics are important because they give an indication of how many people commit suicide. Moreover, since the same agencies gather suicide statistics in the same way, day-in/day-out, they provide a picture of how the numbers committing suicide change over time.

Statisticians can give an indication of which groups of people are "at risk" of committing suicide by examining sociological factors such as: occupation, age, sex, marital status and education.

We turn to suicide statistics to ask, who commits suicide – and why?

Who commits suicide?

In the last decade Britain has seen a 50 percent increase in the number of attempted suicides each year. Every *three minutes* someone will attempt to take their life. Fortunately, not everyone succeeds. Of between 150,000 and 200,000 suicide attempts in Britain every year, over 6,000 result in death. More than 5,000 of these deaths will be by people affected by depression.

Anyone, rich or poor, young or old, male or female, may take their own lives. However, some groups are statistically more likely to succeed than others. Women make three times more suicide attempts than men. However, two thirds of successful suicides are men.

The age of people who successfully kill themselves has changed dramatically in the last thirty years. In 1971, the older you were, the more likely you were to take your own life. Table 1 shows the 1971 suicide rate per 100,000 people in each age group for men and women.

Table 1: suicide rates per 100,000 by sex and age, 1971

Sex/age	15-24	25-44	45-64	>65
Males	6.9	13.5	19.8	25.4
Females	3.3	7.7	15.9	16.5

Table 2 shows that by 2000 the situation had changed. Suicide rates were generally up, although the rates for older men and women were down. The highest rate of suicide was among men aged 25-44.

Table 2: suicide rates per 100,000 by sex and age, 2000

Sex/age	15-24	25-44	45-64	>65
Males	15.9	23.4	18.0	15.7
Females	4.4	6.4	6.3	6.0

Figures 1 and 2 show the trend in the suicide rate from 1971 to 1998. The suicide rate for older women fell dramatically from the mid-1980s to come into line with the suicide rate for younger women. Figure 1 shows the alarming increase in the rate of suicide among males aged 15-24. Although the male, 25-44 age group has the higher rate of suicide, it is the 15-24 age group that has seen the more dramatic increase. If you are young in Britain today, you are most likely to die by your own hand!

Figure 1: the rate of suicide per 100,000 for males by age group, 1971-1998 UK.

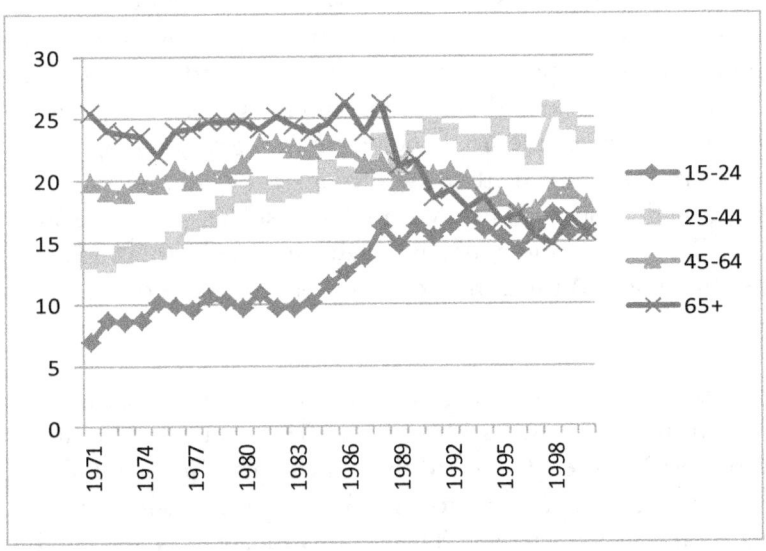

Figure 2: the rate of suicide per 100,000 for females by age group, 1971-1998 UK.

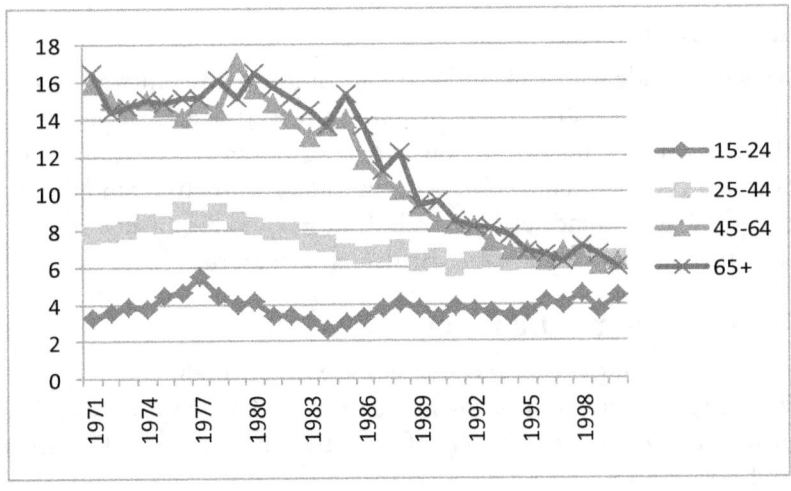

Source: Office for National Statistics; General Register Office for Scotland; Northern Ireland Statistics and Research Agency. Tables 7.15 and 7.22 for *Social Trends 32*.

Suicide and attempted suicide

The picture for attempted suicide among men and women is the reverse of that for successful suicide. Whereas two-thirds of all suicides are men, two-thirds of suicide attempts are by women. The reason for this discrepancy can be explained (in part at least) by the different methods adopted by women and men. Men tend to attempt suicide using "active" methods such as shooting or jumping from high structures. These methods lead to instant death. Women, by contrast, tend to opt for "passive" methods such as overdose and cutting. While these methods can be equally deadly, they tend not to be instantaneous. As such they offer scope for rescue or a change of mind.

There has been some lowering of the priority given to victims of attempted suicide by the health services. To begin with, the label "cry for help" is often applied to these incidents. Implicit in this label is the notion that a "cry for help" is in some way less serious than a "real" suicide attempt. This is unfortunate since the rate of suicide among those attempting suicide is 1 in 100. "The highest risk occurs in the first three years following a suicide attempt, particularly in the first six months". (Donnellan 2000, p5)

Race and suicide

Rates of suicide for black and Asian people are little known, not least because British death certificates do not record details of people's ethnic or cultural identity[1]. Nevertheless, a number of studies have indicated that women (and especially Indian women) from ethnic minority backgrounds are particularly at risk, with a suicide rate of three times that of their white British counterparts.

Suicide and mental illness

Seventy percent of recorded suicides are by people who have experienced depression or manic depression. Between nine and thirteen percent are by people affected by schizophrenia (Department of Health 2001).

---

[1] The Coroners Rules have recently been amended so that race will now be recorded on death certificates. This will provide insights into suicide among ethnic minority groups in future.

It is almost axiomatic that those suffering mental illness should be at high risk of suicide, since suicide is often recorded as having happened to someone of "unsound mind". Indeed, this is an area where one might need to be cautious when interpreting the figures, since the fact that someone had experienced mental illness might inform the suicide verdict – coroners may be more likely to record accidental deaths of people with mental illness as suicides.

While mental illness may increase the risk of suicide among those affected, one might be forgiven for thinking that it might attract a higher level of formal support and that, as such, those at greatest risk might actually be better protected. The last decade has seen a 50 percent increase in the numbers detained under the Mental Health Act. The suicide rate rose during the same period:

"A National Inquiry found that 26% of suicides were by people who had been in contact with mental health services in the last year; 13% of this group were inpatients in a psychiatric hospital at the time of death; 28% had killed themselves within three months of being discharged." (Donnellan 2000, p12)

This shows that psychiatric hospitals do not provide a guarantee against suicide. It also tells us that people discharged from hospital are not necessarily no longer at risk! This should also warn us of the dangers of applying risk assessments to individuals when many of the factors associated with risk are actually social and economic rather than psychological.

Sociological factors and Suicide

Social factors such as marital status, employment status and living circumstances are most accurate predictors of suicide. Table 3 shows the marital status of suicides notified to the National Confidential Inquiry into Suicide and Homicide by People with Mental Illness. (*Safety First*, Department of Health 2001)

Table 3: marital status and suicide in England and Wales

Marital status	Percent
Widowed	7
Divorced/Separated	26
Married/Co-habiting	29
Single	38

Single people are clearly at greater risk of suicide than married people, particularly when one adds those who are divorced or separated to those who are single. However, these statistics may be picking up another factor that is even more important – people's living circumstances. Table 4 shows people's living circumstances prior to their suicide.

Table 4: Living circumstances and suicide in England and Wales

Living circumstance	Percent
Other shared (e.g., friends)	4
Other non-shared	7
With children only	4
With parents	13
With spouse/Partner (with or without children)	29
Alone	43

People living alone make up nearly half of all the cases reported. This seems to be the more important factor than being single, separated or divorced, although many of these people will also be living alone. It is likely that someone affected by extreme stressors and/or mental illness, but lacking close family or friends will find suicide more of an option than someone with close confidants.

Being out of work would seem also to be implicated in suicide. Table 5 shows the employment status of the suicides reported in *Safety First*.

Table 5: Employment status and suicide in England and Wales

Employment status	Percent
Paid employment (including self-employed and part time)	17
Full time student	1
Housewife/husband	8
Retired	10
Long-term sick	18
Unemployed	41
Other	5

Clearly, being out of work, for whatever reason, is a major factor in suicide. The Welsh Health Survey 1998 (National Assembly for Wales) seems to confirm this, drawing the link between poor mental health and unemployment, and highlighting the deterioration in mental health of those who are out of work for prolonged periods.

While we can highlight the importance of social factors in suicide, they are not sufficient causes. Suicide is a far more complex process. Not everyone, most or even many of those who are divorced, separated, single, unemployed, long-term sick or living alone attempt or commit suicide.

We need to be cautious when applying statistics to the assessment of individual risk.

A cautionary note about statistics

As the old adage has it, there are lies, damned lies and statistics. Statistics give an indication of what is going on, they do not provide the full picture. This is particularly true in the case of suicide.

Suicide statistics are notoriously inaccurate. Indeed, university social science departments use suicide statistics to illustrate the difficulties involved in presenting a picture of real-life using numbers gathered by official agencies for purposes other, necessarily than providing such a picture.

Emile Durkheim, one of the founding fathers of modern social science, observed a difference in the suicide rates of protestant and catholic countries, suggesting that catholic countries were more cohesive and better equipped to cope with stress. Contemporary social scientists have taken issue with this. What about catholic Hungary, which has one of the highest suicide rates in Europe? It may well be that differences in suicide rates between catholic and protestant countries could be explained by the different attitudes within such countries, rather than through any difference in the real number of suicides. Since suicide is stigmatised more in catholic than protestant countries, coroners in catholic countries, concerned for the surviving family, would be less likely to record suicide verdicts. Indeed, even within protestant or secular countries, some families may have the resources to persuade coroners not to record suicide verdicts.

The implication of this (as true today as it was when Durkheim was writing) is that suicide statistics cannot predict individual cases. However, they are a potent means of measuring the mental health of society as a whole. As Durkheim (1888) pointed out, a rise in the suicide rate indicates a decline in the well-being of the society.

It is no coincidence that the quarter century 1970 to 1995, which saw such a large increase in the UK suicide rate was also a period of major economic and social upheaval.

What causes suicide?

There used to be a debate about whether human activity resulted from "nature" or "nurture". That is, to ask whether one's behaviour is the result of one's biology or one's upbringing?

In the end, neither side of this debate was terribly convincing. Rather, we had to concede that human behaviour was far more complex than first thought, often involving a combination of biological and social factors as well as being affected by the whole range of immediate life events. With this in mind, one must look at all of those apparent causes of suicide as having to interact in a complicated manner before suicidal behaviour results.

One way of breaking down the various factors that lead to suicidal behaviour is to separate those that are part of a person's make up – *predisposing* factors – from immediate life events – *precipitating* factors.

Predisposing factors

There is strong evidence to suggest that both biology and socialisation play a major part in predisposing people to suicidal behaviour. However, one must be careful not to try to explain suicide in terms of any one factor.

Recent research has shown that a particular gene mutation appears to a significant degree in people who commit suicide (BBC News Online April 2001). Against this, not everyone (or even many) with this gene mutation actually will commit suicide. Furthermore, the majority of those who commit suicide do not carry the mutation. There is no "suicide gene" but there *may* be genetic predispositions.

There is also evidence to suggest that people's upbringing can significantly increase their risk of suicide. People who experienced abuse as children appear in large numbers among those who go on to commit suicide. Similarly, people bullied in childhood are over-represented among the victims of suicide. Once again, though, more abused children survive than go on to kill themselves. Upbringing does not cause suicide, but *may* predispose people to it.

Other, less clear-cut aspects of socialisation may also have an effect on one's chances of dying by suicide. There is evidence to suggest that children who did not receive unconditional love from parents in the first year of life are emotionally ill-equipped to deal with adversity in later life. The children of perfectionist parents may be prone to the kind of "all or nothing thinking" that makes life's setbacks seem like catastrophes and life's successes seem inadequate.

In the end, we need considerably more research into these kinds of apparently predisposing factors to see how, exactly, they interact with other factors to bring about suicidal behaviour. For while one or more of these factors may predispose an individual to suicidal behaviour, even a combination of all of them could not be regarded as sufficient cause of suicide. People with the most horrendous early life experiences can go on to lead happy, healthy lives, while those with little in the way of childhood trauma go on to take their own lives.

Even if one could clearly identify predisposing factors, it is far from clear how much impact any resultant intervention would have on the suicide rate. Of course, there is a value to providing better drugs for conditions resulting from genetic and bio-chemical factors. There may even be a value in developing therapies that attempt to assist people in coming to terms with their unhealthy pasts (although there are those schools of thought that argue that resources are best used to help people deal with their immediate problems and should only be applied to past experiences if these are a major concern to the patient). Nevertheless, it is only by removing and/or mitigating the immediate, *precipitating* factors that underlie suicidal behaviour that one can have any dramatic effect on the suicide rate.

Precipitating factors

Just as some people may be biologically and socially predisposed to suicidal behaviour but never actually attempt suicide, so people who are not predisposed may, given the right combination of stressors, attempt suicide. Furthermore, those predisposed to suicidal behaviour most often have to have precipitating factors to drive them to attempt suicide. Thus, in many ways, it is the precipitating factors that are the most serious causes of suicidal behaviour.

Any list of precipitating factors in suicides and attempted suicides will be long, and will include:

- o Bereavement
- o Unemployment
- o Relationship problems, divorce and separation
- o Bullying/abuse
- o Workplace stress
- o Financial problems
- o Ill-health.

These will often be accompanied by emotional responses within the individual that make them more likely to attempt suicide. These will include:

- Loneliness
- Depression
- Helplessness
- Hopelessness
- Tiredness
- Guilt
- Low self-esteem.

Table 6 shows the percentage of males and females reporting having experienced a range of major life stressors in the year 2000.

Table 6: Prevalence of major life stressors in 2000 by sex.

Life Stressor	Males	Females
Death of a close relative	51	55
Death of a close friend or other relative	68	73
Made redundant or sacked	40	19
Having a serious life-threatening illness or injury	30	22
Separation due to marital difficulties or breakdown of a steady relationship	25	29
Bullying	19	17
Serious money problems	14	8
Violence at work	6	2
Violence at home	4	10
Being Homeless	4	3
Sexual abuse	2	5

Source: Social Trends 32

Table 7 shows the precipitating factors associated with suicide attempts among those completing the charity survey. Given that the respondents were members of the charity, it is of no surprise that stress, depression and related mental health problems were the most prominent causes. A broader survey, perhaps looking at a random sample of those attempting suicide would be more likely to find events like bereavement, separation and divorce as the main factors. Nevertheless, mental illness would be high on any list of factors. Furthermore, the prominence of stress and depression in the charity survey emphasises the point that without appropriate, on-going support, depression is a *killer illness*!

Table 7: Factors precipitating a suicide attempt

Factor	Number	Factor	Number
Stress/mental illness	110	Housing/relocation	11
Relationship/family problems	80	Problems with friends	9
Disability/illness	44	Withdrawal of support	4
Problems at work	33	Stress of being a carer	3
Abuse/bullying	33	Inappropriate professional behaviour	2
Bereavement	23	Prozac[2]	2
Money/unemployment	16	Alcohol	1

Often, it is a person's state of mind when faced with life stressors that will determine suicidal behaviour.

Table 8 shows the emotions that respondents to the charity survey experienced immediately prior to attempting suicide.

---

[2] There is apparently some link between SSRIs and suicide in a tiny minority of cases. Whether this is because they actually cause suicidal or violent behaviour or whether they provide energy to people wishing to end their lives has yet to be established.

Table 8: Precipitating emotional states:

Emotion	Number
Guilt	4
Helplessness	9
Low self-esteem	14
Hopelessness	18
Stigmatised	21
Loneliness	90
Other	6

It may well be that the emotional state experienced by a person immediately prior to a suicide attempt led to irrational thought and action. Someone may feel lonely even when there are many friends and family members ready to provide help and support. Someone may give up hope that things can improve when an objective observer might point out that there is much on which to base hope for the future.

This is where the predisposing and precipitating factors all roll into one to produce suicidal behaviour. Faced with the same stressor, for example bereavement, different people will react in different ways. One person may withdraw, feeling great sadness and loss. Another may call on a network of family and friends to ensure that "life goes on". The reason why the behaviours differ may be to do with each person's upbringing – one being better able to continue with social activities than another. It may be due to the way each person's biochemistry reacts to the trauma of loss. It may be a combination of these factors together with immediate stressors such as, perhaps, concerns about money and housing resulting from the loss of a breadwinner. Unfortunately, it is only when a person reacts to particular events that potential risk becomes manifest. Prior to this, our assessment of risk tends to be little better than guesswork.

Suicide and antidepressants

In recent years there has been a growing public awareness of the link between suicide and antidepressants[3]. In particular, and largely as a

---

[3] Studies since the 1980s have suggested that antidepressants may cause suicide in

result of court cases in the USA, the drugs Prozac and Seroxat have been accused of causing suicidal behaviour. That is, that someone who had not been inclined to suicidal behaviour would become suicidal solely because they had taken an antidepressant.

This may be true in an extremely small number of cases. However, given that persistent thoughts of suicide are common to depression, and that people affected by depression are at significant risk of suicidal behaviour, it is difficult to establish that any suicidal behaviour would not have occurred anyway, or that the person was not keeping quiet about their suicidal inclinations. Indeed, it may be that the increased energy brought about by taking an antidepressant may increase people's ability to act on their suicidal thoughts.

More research is needed to determine if there is a causal link between antidepressants and suicide. In the meantime, we need to be cautious about making changes to prescribing practices. There are many areas of medicine where a small number of deaths are tolerated because of the wider benefits. Furthermore, there is little available in the way of a credible alternative to SSRIs in the treatment of moderate-severe depression.

Older, tricyclic antidepressants such as dothiepin and amitriptyline are highly toxic in small overdoses. As table 9 shows, these two drugs are responsible for the majority of antidepressant-related self-poisonings. The phasing out of these drugs in favour of SSRIs has brought about a steady decline in the overall number of antidepressant-related deaths similar to the results of restricting the supply of Paracetamol (see figure 3).

---

some cases. (see for example Mann, JJ and Kapur S. 1991; Gunell D. and Frankel, S. 1994; Hegardy 1995)

Table 9: Number of deaths where antidepressants were mentioned on the death certificate in England and Wales, 1997-2001:

	1997	1998	1999	2000	2001
Dothiepin	262	244	219	201	170
Amitriptyline	177	183	162	142	118
All MAOIs	9	5	4	2	1
All SSRIs	34	34	57	70	95
Total	539	510	493	449	416

Source: Office of National Statistics, *Health Statistics Quarterly 17*, Spring 2003

Figure 3: Number of deaths where Paracetamol and antidepressants were mentioned on the death certificate, England and Wales 1997-2001:

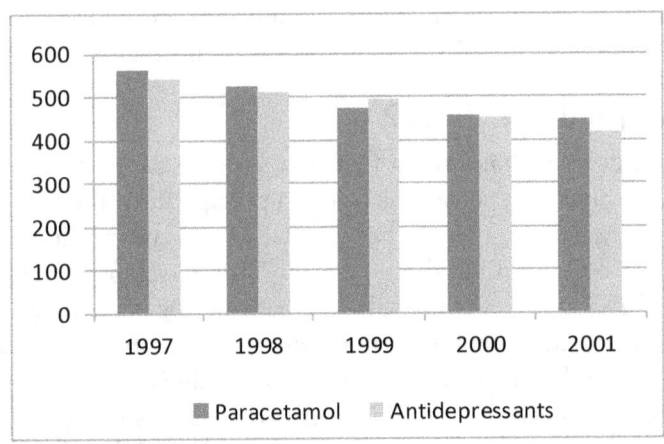

Source: Office of National Statistics, *Health Statistics Quarterly 17*, Spring 2003

It would be no more acceptable in suicide prevention terms to decrease the use of SSRIs in favour of tricyclics than it would be to remove the current restrictions on the availability of Paracetamol.

Furthermore, restricting the means of suicide is not the same as having an overall strategy. Although it is common for depressed people to be given antidepressants and then be left to their own devices, this goes against available guidelines.

People with mild-moderate depression should not be given antidepressants alone as a first line of treatment. As the British National Formulary points out:

"Antidepressant drugs are not generally effective in milder forms of acute depression but a trial may be considered in cases refractory to psychological treatments."(2002, p187)

One would assume that those administering psychological treatments would pick up any changes in condition and/or any problems with the medication. On the other hand, those with the more severe depression for which antidepressants are particularly effective should expect to receive much greater levels of support, including the monitoring of any risk of suicide or attempted suicide.

In short, then, antidepressant suicides, whether triggered by the medication or using the medication as a means, are as much a failure of care services as a problem with the medication itself.

Can we predict suicide?

There is a danger of assuming that because we can see that those who succeed in suicide were "at risk" due to precipitating and/or predisposing factors, that we can predict who actually will kill themselves by examining these factors. Those looking at genes have suggested that it may be possible to create "anti-suicide drugs" that could be targeted at people with genetic predisposition to suicide. There has also been a growing belief in the value of preventative detention as a means of removing potential victims from the means of suicide. We should remember, however, that while it is possible to identify *groups* of people who are at risk of suicide, it is impossible to deal with any certainty in *individual* cases.

In fact, 85 percent of those people who killed themselves who were seen by medical practitioners in England and Wales between 1996 and 2001 were classed as either no-risk or low-risk. Only 5 percent were thought to be high-risk (Department of Health 2001). Thus, even highly sensitised professionals working in a mental health system that is increasingly concerned with risk and the threat of litigation are unable to predict suicide.

Where an examination of statistical risk and causal factors *is* useful is in cutting through some common misconceptions about suicide. The first misconception, and most abused by health and social services professionals, is that most suicide attempts are *merely* a "cry for help". The fact that risk increases dramatically as the number of instances of harming and suicidal behaviour increases suggests that *any* self-harming and/or suicidal behaviour must be taken seriously.

The second misconception is that suicide is only a risk to weak-minded people. Often it is the stereotypical strong, silent types whose bottling up of feelings will put them at most risk when faced with major adversity.

Perhaps the biggest myth that suicide statistics explode is that suicide only affects other people. For, in truth, the suicide victim is everyman. Given the right combination of stressors and a high enough sense of powerlessness, any one of us might be driven to suicidal behaviour.

The real point coming out of the statistical data is that all of us have a vested interest in seeing suicide reduced – for personal as well as altruistic reasons.

How Does It Feel?

Life was so black I truly wanted to die. A living hell, the guilt was so heavy. People's comments, saying that people who commit suicide are selfish only thinking about themselves, one carries the guilt even more. Ignorance is bliss. The negative power that takes over the mind is so powerful. "Death Wish", yes, please get me out of this hell – no more pain, no more black, black days – heaven has just got to be a nicer place. –Survey respondent.

Cold statistics may convey something of the risk of suicide. Only the testimony of those who have been suicidal can give some insight into the experience. The survey into suicide focused mainly on gathering statistics. However, many of the respondents added their experiences and returned these with their questionnaires. As a result, we have been able to get some insight into what it is like to experience such despair that ending one's life not only appears as a rational option, but as the *only* option.

Suicidal emotions

The survey identified a range of emotions tied up with respondents' suicide attempts. These included:

- o Loneliness
- o Stigma
- o Hopelessness
- o Low self-esteem
- o Helplessness
- o Guilt.

Loneliness, and the feeling that no-one could understand how it feels was a common theme:

In the last 15 years I have often thought about committing suicide due to loneliness and depression, but I knew I couldn't because I love my daughter too much to do that to her. When I did try, it was totally out of the blue. I was so tired I did not know what to do with myself. I crawled into bed and thought, 'I've had enough of all this', and reached out for my bottle of tablets. I fell asleep while I was deciding, and when I woke up next morning the bottle was in my hand. I wish I had done it and not gone to sleep instead...

The loneliness experienced by those who attempt suicide is often a personal isolation. On the outside, they are members of families and friendship groups. They go to work, and mix with colleagues. But inside, in spite of the crowd, they are alone:

The isolation I felt prior to my suicide attempt was chronic. Not physical isolation, but mental. My thoughts became disordered and I was not thinking properly. I became very agitated and anxious, especially in the few days before my suicide attempt. I did not know what was wrong with me and I was in a constant state of fear while at the same time trying to carry on "as normal" i.e., going to work, etc...

However, sometimes the isolation is real. The discrimination and lack of understanding surrounding mental illness makes it extremely difficult for the affected person to talk about their concerns:

To live with depression, in my case manic depression, for the bulk of one's life, being unable to discuss the illness openly due to the stigma attached and perhaps more so because the public generally are so unaware of the illness that discussion with them is impossible, means at most times having to bear the illness and its repercussions alone. Even family members do not begin to understand the illness and how you may behave...

Discrimination can be a particular problem for men. Our cultural expectation that "big boys shouldn't cry" prevents men from talking about their feelings. This is reflected in the rising suicide rate among young and middle-aged men.

I feel the media's image of men is a big problem. Young men don't talk about emotional/mental problems to each other, and those with depression are then having feelings of inadequacy. I don't know the answer but it's a big problem and it's getting worse.

Often the emotions associated with depression are all mixed up. The combination of guilt, loneliness, hopelessness and helplessness combining to make the desire for oblivion all too powerful:

When I attempted suicide, I truly believed my family would be better off without me as I was behaving so strangely. At that time I felt that the doctors I saw had no understanding of how desperate I felt. It may have been because I wasn't capable of describing exactly how I felt...

Nor does this emotional turmoil have to relate to damaging objective circumstances. Indeed, when suicides and suicide attempts occur, they often come as a surprise to those close to the victim:

I felt I couldn't cope any more with work, friends or family. I was lonely and felt that no one would understand how I felt. I couldn't understand it myself. I have a job, my own house, a car, etc, what do I have to be miserable about? These were all thoughts that went through my mind. But I'd had enough and suicide seemed the only way out. I even failed at that. The hardest feeling to overcome afterward is the feeling of guilt.

Perhaps the saddest aspect of the stories told by the respondents to our survey is that just being able to talk, and to begin to come to terms with the emotions associated with suicide, is often enough to prevent suicidal thoughts becoming suicidal actions. Unfortunately, the isolation felt and experienced by many respondents meant that they were driven to attempt suicide on more than one occasion.

Multiple suicide attempts

In the last chapter we saw how the risk of suicide increases as people make repeated suicide attempts. Alarmingly, then, many of our respondents report having attempted suicide on numerous occasions – often in spite of being in regular contact with statutory mental health services:

My attempts at suicide became increasingly serious, but I was not taken seriously until I took a serious overdose that left me with liver and kidney failure and critically ill. Until then, family and doctors thought I was being manipulative and trying to get sympathy.

Between November 1997 and April 2000 I took 13 overdoses. The overdose prior to my final one, I had eventually died, and had to be resuscitated, but I still took an overdose about three weeks later, but smaller. The time I died and was resuscitated, I had desperately wanted to die because of the mental, physical and sexual abuse and torture I had suffered in the past.

One tragic theme running through many of the stories related by those of our respondents who had a history of multiple suicide attempts was of a lack of understanding and support on the part of those professionals who should have recognised the signs of people in severe distress, and who failed to act appropriately:

At university, I was severely depressed, suffering from bulimia and inflicting self-harm. I summoned courage to visit the university counsellor, who told me that I could not receive sessions for two months as I could not be fitted in, despite the fact I told her I felt extremely suicidal and had planned how to do it. She told me to visit the doctor, who put me on Prozac and sent me home. My first suicide attempt was prevented by friends who took me to casualty where they established that I hadn't taken any Paracetamol, and promptly sent me home. The following evening I lay in ICU, having taken 50 Paracetomol with three bottles of wine. I was seen by the on-duty psychiatrist, who assessed from a few stupid questions that I no longer posed a risk to myself, and as soon as my liver function was stable, I was released. I returned home to Northampton with my parents, and was seen by another psychiatrist whose manner was extremely cold and lacked understanding, which did not encourage me to open up. He misdiagnosed me, and I was sent to the wrong unit, only to be re-referred back to the psychiatrist. I then endured three months of assessments with various consultants only to be told, since I was returning to university to complete my degree, there was no use in offering me any treatment, and I should return to my GP if I felt it still necessary once my studies had finished!? This left me feeling frustrated and that my suicide attempt and the pain I was still suffering was not taken seriously. Even though I now work for a mental health trust, I would be very reluctant to ask for help from the NHS – the reason I am still alive is definitely not due to them!

The themes of lack of understanding and inappropriate professional behaviour were sadly prominent in the stories of our respondents. Far from helping people overcome their suicidal feelings, and helping them overcome the depression that brought them about, the medical profession had become another of the problems leading to suicide.

This can start at the point of contact with the NHS, in an A&E department following self-harm or a suicide attempt:

> *Hospital casualty staff were unkind, unhelpful and not willing to hear what I was trying to say. I was treated like a huge inconvenience and waste of time[4].*

It is perhaps understandable that members of a profession whose purpose is to save life should feel resentment toward people who deliberately try to end their own lives. It is also likely that the volume of work demanded of staff in a modern A&E department prevents them from appearing concerned and sympathetic.

Nevertheless, when dealing with an attempted suicide, to patch up the physical scars without attending to the mental distress is an insufficient response. If someone has attempted suicide once, they are likely to try again. And it is not only the distressed individual who is at risk:

> *I first contemplated suicide when I was 30, even to the point of taking my son and daughter's lives when they were aged three and one respectively...*

Barely a month goes by without a British newspaper carrying a story of someone whose suicide involved taking the lives of their families as well as their own. We cannot, therefore, treat self-harm and suicide attempts as *merely* "attention seeking" or *just* "a cry for help".

---

[4] It should have been standard practice for anyone who had attempted suicide to be referred to the duty psychiatrist prior to discharge from an A&E department.

Long-term care

Mental illness is more a process than an incident. For many people, the experience is of varying degrees of distress and disability throughout their lives. This raises difficulties for those involved in the long-term care of people with mental illness.

There are problems with the compartmentalisation of services. This happens both between service providers and within services provided by the same agency.

Services are often allocated on the basis of availability rather than need. With a shortage of around 500 consultant psychiatrists in the UK, and similar shortages of other mental health professionals, services tend to be allocated by illness rather than severity of condition[5]. The result is that mental health has become more an emergency-only service than one able to intervene to promote mental health and ward off severe illness.

Those affected by mental illness often find that their needs are translated into available services. Thus, a person may be told that they "need" antidepressants, or psychotherapy or inpatient psychiatric care. However, what the person may actually *need* is a wide range of interventions to help them manage their lives at a time when their mental health is impaired. For example, they may *need* support in dealing with the benefits system, or with housing. They may *need* a lawyer to help them sue an employer for workplace stress or unfair dismissal. They may *need* counselling to help with relationship problems, or to assist them in making a decision about stressful employment. It is often these non-medical needs that people affected by mental illness see as most urgent:

> *Some questions are difficult to isolate like this – clinical depression has many inter-linked components, i.e., money problems → stress → insomnia → anxiety. Too many problems with side effects → fear, lack of ability to cope.*

---

[5] The fact that National Assembly for Wales guidance has told practitioners not to prioritise services in this way demonstrates that the practice has been happening to a degree that has prompted governmental intervention.

Because formal mental health services only address some of what people need, and because these needs tend to be addressed on the basis of availability of services, people can find themselves caught in a revolving door in which unsupported discharges from hospital result in a failure to cope that, in turn, lead to a new admission to hospital:

> *Vicious cycle... the TV/media still seem to say its 'easily' treatable, just finding the right drug – in hospital lack of continuity of carers (or abuse). Lack of resources when going home – back to the same problems: over-stretched, under-resourced community care.*

Nor are hospitals necessarily able to offer the most appropriate levels of care. Indeed, people receiving community-based services often have more one-to-one contact with support workers than do hospital inpatients:

> *I had been in mental hospital for about four months when I tried to put my fingers in a light socket. I had good support from the staff but they were far too thin on the ground and seldom able/available to talk to patients when we feel we needed them most. People used to talk to the cleaners about their symptoms, as it was much easier.*

The pressures placed on staff within the NHS are not new. Nor are they restricted to mental health services. Indeed, it is the same kinds of pressures in A&E departments that tend to grab the headlines. However, in the mental health setting these pressures are the more worrying because the most effective "treatment" of mental illness is often face-to-face "talking therapy".

Most tragically, services seem so over-stretched that they cannot act in a preventative way even for those people already in the system. Indeed, statistically, the more contact you have with formal mental health services, the more likely you are to succeed in killing yourself:

> *The second time I tried to kill myself I had been in the system for years already, and several, some long, hospital admissions and years of day hospital. I have a good GP and psychiatrist (and now a psychologist).*

Yet somehow when I became even more severely depressed – apart from hospital again – the system does not seem able to offer more to get you through a crisis. There is no slack in the system or anything else they can offer – even short term – to get you through it. Professionals are not always available when help is urgently needed – even to talk – even if I could have. When nothing in me ever changes, and the only option would be maybe to be sectioned again, I feel so alone and to be dead is a very acceptable option. I have been medically retired for 5 years now due to my illness and feel that despite everyone's best efforts for 13 years, I'm not really any further forward. Aspects of my illness have changed but really I've still not been able to leave the starting blocks on the road to getting better.

Like much else in the modern NHS, the services aimed at those experiencing mental distress are overstretched and under-resourced. All too often, people in distress are met by an emergency-only service that patches them up, but cannot cure them.

The time and attention needed to deal with the emotional side of the severe depression that often leads to suicide is beyond the NHS. The practical support needed to help people overcome the life changes that bring about depression is fragmented and out of reach. This is not simply a matter of finance – although considerable increases in funding across mental health services are needed. Key professions such as psychiatrists, psychiatric nurses and GPs have high numbers of vacancies which may take a decade or more to fill. Furthermore, there are a wide range of patient needs that do not fall into conventional definitions of services for which new approaches have to be developed.

For the foreseeable future, the kind of pain and distress set out in this chapter will continue to increase. Simultaneously, the capacity of health and social care services to deal with its results will continue to diminish (even if considerable increases in funding are secured).

In chapter four we look at how the state has sought to lower the suicide rate, and why these approaches have failed. In chapter five we look at alternative approaches.

A Problem for Individuals?

In September 2002 the Department of Health announced a new *National Suicide Prevention Strategy for England*. That Government has produced a strategy is to be welcomed. It is also worth noting that the strategy recognises the need for a broad approach that looks at issues such as mental health promotion. However, much of the strategy repeats the previous approach taken by successive governments in focussing on preventative detention and removing the means of suicide from individuals in the care of the NHS and prisons.

The trouble is that this approach has been tried by successive governments with little overall success.

The temptation to focus on a particular population sub-group within those who kill themselves is great. The current Government has chosen to target young men. However, unless new initiatives are given new resources, we will see a diversion of resources from other at-risk groups, leading to an increase in their suicide rates. This appears to have happened over the last twenty years when the focus was on cutting suicide among older people (see figures 1 and 2, above). Furthermore, a failure to tackle the underlying causes of suicide, will result in a failure to achieve what should be the main objective – a lowering of the overall rate of suicide.

On a smaller scale, the Government proposes to extend measures to remove the means of suicide. It has already succeeded in cutting the number of paracetamol suicides by cutting the number of tablets that can be sold at any one time. But this success has had little impact on the overall rate of suicide. Thus, while the Government is correct to note that such initiatives can successfully prevent "impulse suicides", by failing to address the desire for suicide, these initiatives often lead to alternative methods being used later on. Thus, while death by paracetamol has decreased, death by hanging has increased proportionately so that the overall suicide rate has fallen only slightly.

The economic prosperity of the late 1990s will have had a much greater impact on the suicide rate than the government restriction on paracetamol sales. This is borne out by recent reports that many retail outlets do not stick to the restrictions on paracetamol, suggesting that it is far easier to purchase enough for an overdose than government has been claiming. It is also borne out by an examination of regional variations in suicide rate which, if government claims on the effectiveness of the paracetamol restrictions were true, would suggest that the paracetomol sold in Scotland and Wales is significantly more toxic than that sold in England! Of course, the more rational explanation is that the economic prosperity that has resulted in a huge influx of population into the southeast of England since the mid-1990s is also responsible for the drop in the suicide rate (outside London) in that region. Meanwhile, regions like Scotland, Wales and the north of England have seen less economic prosperity and more social fragmentation (not least by losing skilled professionals to the southeast), and in consequence have seen suicide rates remain high.

Brock, et al (2006), presenting official statistics on suicide, are quite clear that regional variations in the suicide rate correlate with deprivation

This suggests that government initiatives based on withdrawing the means of suicide from suicidal individuals are more likely to result in suicide displacement rather than suicide reduction. It is inconceivable that we could remove every possible means of suicide from the public. Where the demand is strong enough, the means will be found.

This is not to suggest that removing obvious means of suicide should not be attempted. The change from coal gas to natural gas, curbing the supply of paracetamol and the introduction of catalytic converters have all served to prevent suicides, particularly so-called "impulse suicides". However, removing means without removing desire can only have partial success. Without addressing the wider reasons for suicide, restricting means is unlikely to have much of an impact on the overall suicide rate.

Suicide as a disease of individuals

Insofar as it is individuals that kill themselves, it is not unreasonable for medical practitioners to treat those believed to be at risk. It does not follow, however, that attempts to lower the *rate* of suicide should also focus on these individuals. This would be like running a crime prevention programme that focused on existing criminals without addressing why they and other people may take to crime in the first place.

Historically public policy has been punitive toward those who attempt suicide and to the families of those who succeed. The UK was one of the last democracies to decriminalise suicide – it ceased to be a crime in 1961. Even so, mental health legislation has continued to treat those thought to be at risk of killing themselves in the same way as those thought to be at risk of killing others, taking no account of the individual's capacity and imposing a regime based on detention and compulsion.

In recent years government has allowed those deemed to be at risk of suicide to be detained, continuously supervised and compelled to receive treatment. It is in this vein that *Safety First* recommends that: "in-patient wards... remove or cover all likely ligature points, including all non-collapsible curtain rails." (Department of Health 2001, p10). These recommendations have now been incorporated into the *National Suicide Prevention Strategy for England*. Given one of our respondents' attempts to end life by putting her fingers in an electric light socket, one wonders whether removing lighting from hospital wards might be recommended in future! One also wonders about the effect on wheelchair users, as if potential ligature points were removed from disabled toilets, this would render them unusable!

An individual risk based approach might be reasonable if we could meet two criteria:

o   We could predict with some degree of certainty which people were going to attempt suicide, and
o   We could provide meaningful treatment which restored them to an active life in the community (as opposed to

detaining them in a secure bubble in which the means of suicide are removed, but the desire and the mental distress that underpins it remains).

However, even if we could do this, we would need to remove the discrimination associated with this kind of practice. A key reason why people do not seek treatment for mental illness is the fear that they are going mad and, consequently, that they will be taken away and locked up – the persistence of antiquated Victorian asylum buildings does nothing to combat this view. Such people do not (often) get better, they simply turn up at a later date with severe illness or as suicide or attempted suicide statistics.

The problem of prediction

The first difficulty to arise is that our current levels of expertise make it difficult to predict who is at risk of suicide. Predictability is an essential part of any claim to be scientific. In natural sciences we expect absolute predictability. In the human sciences we have come to accept that prediction will have an element of variance. Nevertheless, we do expect to be able to make predictions that are better than guess work – no matter how much experience is brought to bear.

As we have seen, most of the factors associated with suicide tend to be social rather than individual:

- o Unemployment/redundancy
- o Bereavement
- o Divorce/separation
- o Debt
- o Homelessness.

While we can read back from suicide to show that people in these categories were more at risk than the population at large, we cannot turn this around and say that *all* or *any particular* people within these categories will commit suicide:

"There is no single, readily identifiable, high risk population that constitutes a sizeable proportion of overall suicides and yet represents a small, easily targeted group... The prevention paradox, whereby there is disadvantage to the many from interventions that can benefit only the few, is important in a condition as common as ischaemic heart disease. The concern must be all the greater where the outcome to be prevented is as rare as suicide." (Gunnell and Frankel 1994)

Since we cannot compulsorily detain or remove the means of suicide from, for example, every unemployed young male affected by depression, who lives alone, and has expressed a desire to end his life – even though such a person would clearly be in one of the highest risk groups – how else are we to decide who should be detained?

The stock answer in various official documents has been that we must trust in the judgement of professionals working in the field[6].

Policy makers imply that there is some esoteric knowledge among professionals working in mental health services that allows them to know whether someone is at risk prior to that person carrying out any indicative action. There is not. Prediction of individual suicides is shown to be a risky business in the high rate of "true negatives" – cases where the experts have judged that there is little or no risk of suicide, but where the individual goes on to commit suicide. If prediction was any more scientific than guess work, one would assume that less than 50 percent of suicides would have been deemed to be low-risk or no-risk. In fact, a staggering 85 percent of successful suicides who had been in contact with the mental health professions in the three months prior to their deaths were deemed to be no-risk or low-risk. Of these, 48 percent had been seen in the seven days prior to their deaths! (Home Office 2001)

Given that the system errs on the side of safety, we can infer from the high number of true negative cases an even higher number of false positives. The response has not been a re-examination of the belief that suicide is predictable, and hence preventable, in

---

[6] Current legislation allows for detention on the say so of two doctors, to be confirmed later by a psychiatrist. Recent proposals would allow detention on the say so of a much broader range of mental health workers including social workers and nurses.

individuals. Rather, it has prompted calls for *even more* compulsory treatment, *even more* detention, and *even more* supervision.

These calls have opened up the whole question of whether it is moral for us to be detaining even more people "for their own good".

Moral problems

By focusing on those perceived to be at risk of harming or killing themselves, we have allowed mental health legislation to be used as a form of preventative detention. In the case of those detained because they are deemed to be a risk to themselves, we are not talking about a serious crime; we are not talking about a crime at all. Neither suicide nor self-harm are criminal acts.

We might equally reasonably apply preventative detention to people who smoke, people who drink and people who eat red meat, on the grounds that all of these practices are harmful and may result in the premature death of the individual. Suicide is no less fatal, it is just more immediate. We might even add those who drive cars on the grounds that this carries the additional risk of harming others.

We routinely allow people to harm themselves in all manner of ways. Furthermore, outside of mental illness, the state protects an individual's right to refuse treatment even where this will result in death.

In the case of physical illness, we accept treatment without consent only where a patient is incapable of making a decision. For example, a doctor may treat without consent an unconscious accident victim. If, however, the accident victim regains consciousness and asks that the doctor stop, the doctor will be guilty of assault if he or she continues. A Jehovah's Witness may refuse a blood transfusion even though death will be inevitable, without anyone having the right to administer it compulsorily.

Someone who has a diagnosis of a mental illness has no legal right to refuse detention and compulsory treatment. The reason for this is the historical assumption that people with diagnoses of mental illness are unable to make decisions for themselves. This is seldom true.

Even where people lack capacity in one area of life, they remain capable in other areas. By failing to acknowledge this, the law applied to mental illness is, itself, discriminatory and stigmatising, and works as a deterrent to people seeking help.

Ultimately, the moral question is which is likely to bring about a reduction in the overall rate of suicide – more or less detention and/or compulsion? While compulsion may save individual lives, the quasi-penal nature of the mental health system deters many others from seeking help at an early stage. As such, it may contribute to suicide in those not currently in contact with mental health services.

The risk is that the more punitive and autocratic the mental health system is perceived to be, the more individuals will seek to avoid contact with it. This, in turn, means that fewer people seek early interventions, and more people become suicidal prior to seeking support. So a system that saves the lives of a few puts many more at risk.

Practical problems

In the end, the real test of current approaches to suicide reduction is not whether they are moral, but whether they work. That is, has there been a fall in the suicide rate? Irrespective of the moral and scientific problems, if current approaches do not work, we must reject them.

The Government is probably right to suggest that removing the means of suicide can result in reductions in suicide (although this has been overstated). But this cannot be the mainstay of a suicide reduction policy. Government must address the discrimination and lack of public understanding of mental illness; it must tackle the social and economic factors that create suicide risk; it must use the education system to promote emotional intelligence and, most urgently, it must change the mental health services from the Cinderella of the NHS to the priority high quality service that Government says they should be.

The real problem for many people, as our respondents' testimony shows, is not that Government has to work hard to remove the means of suicide from people or remove such people to places of safety. The real problem is that too many suicidal individuals are turned away at the hospital door because the NHS lacks the resources to care for them.

The lack of care in the community leaves people to become seriously ill, but hospitals are already full of seriously ill people, and cannot accommodate even more suicidal patients. Removing ligature points from hospitals may prevent those inside from killing themselves, but it does nothing for those turned away at the hospital gates. The latest Government strategy will need to be watched in this respect because there is a danger that it could become an "embarrassing-only" suicide reduction policy, concerned with those within public sector institutions but unconcerned with those left to die alone in the community. Government must be held to the broader targets that it has set itself.

There is, perhaps, one other reason for rejecting an approach to suicide that uses the judgement of medical practitioners to decide which individuals are at risk, which get treatment and which get detained: doctors themselves have the highest suicide rate and the highest rates of mental illness of all professions in the UK. If doctors are unable to recognise risk in themselves, why should we trust their judgement in relation to others? On the issue of suicide we may rightly say, "physician, heal thyself!"

If we are to curb the suicide rate, we must broaden our focus. This does not mean the removal of services from those with severe and enduring mental illness, nor does it mean abandoning attempts to measure risk and treating those who lack capacity, but it does mean allocating resources to preventative and educative approaches.

Rather than looking at mental *illness*, we need to examine the issue of mental *health*. This means addressing the social factors that cause ill health. It means looking at what we, as individuals and communities, can do to stay healthy, and it means looking at how we rehabilitate those who have experienced mental illness.

Beyond individual ill health

Everyone has mental health needs, whether or not they have a diagnosis of mental illness. These needs are met, or not met, at home, at work, on the streets, in prisons and hospitals, in schools and neighbourhoods – where people feel respected, included and safe, or on the margins, in fear and excluded. Because everyone has mental health needs, the need for mental health promotion is universal and of relevance to everyone. Mental health promotion does have a role in preventing mental health problems, notably anxiety, depression, drug and alcohol dependence and suicide. But mental health promotion also has a wider range of health and social benefits. These include improved physical health, increased emotional resilience, greater social inclusion and participation and higher productivity. – Department of Health 2002.

One of the first academics to think about suicide was Emile Durkheim (1888). Durkheim saw the rate of suicide as a mark of the health of a society. A stable suicide rate was a mark of good health, while a rising rate was a sign that things were going wrong.

The UK suicide rate remained relatively stable throughout the twentieth century. However, between 1974 and 1998 there was a steady rise in the rate of suicide. This rise has been particularly severe in men, and particularly among the young, although this is offset in the overall rate by falls among older people.

This rise cannot be explained by reference to human biology or genetics alone – the birth rate has been falling for several decades. If suicide were hereditary, there would have been an equivalent fall in the suicide rate. In fact, the rate of mental illness and suicide rose from the mid-1970s.

Nevertheless, psychiatry and government policy have tended to focus on the biology/pathology of individuals affected by mental illness, rather than looking at the whole picture.

By focusing on the medical needs of supposedly "at risk" individuals, we tend to miss the wider picture. Rather than asking, "What can we do to prevent individuals taking their own lives?" we need to ask, "why is the suicide rate rising?" and, "why is it rising among particular social groups?"

Such questions have to be asked of society as a whole. But what social factors might explain the increase in the suicide rate?

Anomie revisited

Durkheim argued that the suicide rate rose along with the degree of "anomie" or "normlessness" in any society. Put another way, a period of social upheaval is likely to result in an increase in the suicide rate.

There are, however, some exceptions. In the Great War of 1914-18 suicide rates fell to an all-time low, and the global war of 1939-45 saw a similar fall in suicide rates. The 1920s and 1930s, in contrast, saw an increase in the UK suicide rate, peaking in 1935.

One explanation for this is that while wars are traumatic, they actually result in greater social cohesion (Wilkinson 1996). By contrast, the 1920s saw considerable cultural and social change as the "lost generation" began to reject the Victorian values that had led to the slaughter of millions on the battlefields of Europe.

The fact that it is cultural and social change that results in a rise in the suicide rate, rather, necessarily, than economic or military upheaval, should stand as a warning to those who look for simplistic, and often politically inspired explanations for suicide. When one looks at the factors common to high-risk groups, one must guard against simply labelling these as sufficient causes.

Conservative governments?

Historical trends in suicide rates in Australia and Britain suggest a correlation between Conservative governments and increases in suicide rates (Shaw et al 2002). The period of almost unbroken conservative rule in the UK between 1920 and 1940 saw high suicide rates with a peak in 1935. Similarly, Conservative governments between 1951 and 1964 also presided over rises in the suicide rate, while Labour governments in the 1940s, 1960s and 1970s saw lower rates. Suicide rates rose again in the 1980s and 1990s.

In fact, the analysis is crude. The highest suicide rate in the twentieth century was recorded for the years 1961 to 1965, the last two years of which were presided over by a Labour government. Similarly, falls in the late 1990s actually occurred in the last years of the Conservative government. The 1997 Labour government presided over an increase in the suicide rate in its first two years. Meanwhile, the lowest peacetime suicide rates were recorded under two Conservative governments, the Balfour government of 1902-1906 and the Heath government of 1970-1974.

Nor does the analysis take account of the vast social change across a century in which Britain went from the industrial great power at the heart of the World's largest empire to a post-industrial bit player in a European economic union and a USA-led military alliance. It is difficult to make the case that there were exact parallels in policy or prevailing social conditions between, say, the National (Conservative-led) Government of the mid-1930s to the Thatcher Government of the 1980s.

Rather than giving an explanation of suicide rates, the historical data raise important questions. Most obviously, why do wars create a drop in suicide rates? and what is it about the 1930s that brought about so high an increase? The most obvious answer to these questions concerns *social cohesion*. War tends to create a sense of common interest and common purpose that does not prevail in peacetime. On the other hand, peaks in the suicide rate – 1926-1940 and 1981-1985 – correspond to periods of unemployment, social change and dislocation[7].

---

[7] The exception to this is the peak in the early 1960s. However, this is precisely the example of where statistics can be misleading. Comparing historical rates for anything from vegetable sales to murder to suicide relies on the statistics being recorded in the same way. However, until 1961, suicide was illegal and resulted in punitive action against the victim's family. After 1961, coroners would have responded to the change in the law by being more prepared to give suicide verdicts safe in the knowledge that no legal sanction would be taken against the family. However, given the continuing social stigma, it is likely that within a few years,

Unemployment

Unemployment is not a sufficient cause of suicide. However, unemployment is a major cause of depression, and clearly impacts on the suicide rate.

Williams (1997) argues that unemployment is less of a factor in the suicide rate when it is caused by mass redundancy rather than individual lay-offs. In areas where a large employer closes, the suicide rate often remains stable. There may be a similar localised social cohesion similar to that seen in wartime in these circumstances. The sense that "we are all in it together" may well protect against suicide.

The Welsh Health Survey (1998) shows that it is long-term unemployment that increases the risk of suicide. This would fit in with Williams' (1997) argument, since the immediate social cohesion surrounding mass redundancies may well dissipate in the long term as some people find other work.

Returning to the findings in *Safety First* (2001) it may be the social isolation and social exclusion that often results from long-term economic inactivity that raises the suicide rate rather than economic inactivity itself. This would clearly have implications for the way we respond to events such as plant closures and large scale redundancies. The tendency is to offer support at the point of closure. However, it maybe that the appropriate time to intervene would be some 6-9 months after closure, when the sense of common purpose has dissipated, and when most of those laid-off have found alternative employment.

Consumer society

It is all too easy for us to assume that the way we live today is the way things have always been. It isn't. Home ownership is a feature of the late 20th century. Before the 1939-45 war, leisure activities were limited to such things as going to the football and an annual trip to the seaside. Indeed, walking in the countryside only became lawful

coroners will have allowed themselves to return to open and accidental death verdicts when taking into account the effect on bereaved families.

after the war. Hobsbawm (1990) notes that the first mass consumption product came at the turn of the century with the publication of the "1d *Daily Mail*". Television use only rose among ordinary people from the late 1960s (and even then, rental was the norm before the 1980s).

The unemployment of the 1930s took place within an "industrial society". That is, most ordinary people did not take part in mass consumption beyond those items needed to maintain themselves:

o   Home ownership was increasing among the middle classes, but remained rare among ordinary people
o   Car ownership was the preserve of the rich
o   TV had yet to be made available to the masses, with most people relying on radio and newsreel for their news
o   Fashion came second, a long way behind utility in clothing and furniture.

The economy of the day was geared to mass production, often of industrial capital goods rather than consumer durables. Today's mass consumption industries – electrical goods, cars, etc, only developed in Britain from the late 1930s and only became widely consumed from the late 1950s.

For those living in areas that grew up around single, large-scale industries such as coal, ship building and steel, unemployment tended to affect everyone. Moreover, unlike the closures of the 1980s, redundancies in these industries were temporary – people had the expectation that they would return to their jobs once demand picked up.

Keeping up with the Joneses was relatively easy as most neighbours worked in the same industries, earned similar incomes, and shopped in the same stores. This, in turn, fostered a greater sense of social cohesion.

But if the society of the 1930s was about keeping up with the Joneses, today's might be more about keeping up with the Beckhams. Manufacturing industry today takes second place to those industries and services concerned with mass consumption. Mass communications fuel and are fuelled by mass consumption. People's lifestyle expectations rise accordingly. Furthermore, people have come to measure their self-esteem and worth according to the lifestyles they are able to maintain. In modern society, people are encouraged to buy:

- The most expensive house they can borrow for
- The most expensive car they can borrow for
- The most expensive furniture and fashions they can borrow for.

Many of us have become materialist to the point that we measure our own self-worth according to the value of our possessions. In such circumstances, unemployment not only results in severe financial problems, it also shatters all the trappings of self-worth. Moreover, the trend toward social fragmentation in which fewer of us even speak to our neighbours or engage with our local communities means that when life shaking events like redundancy do happen, far too many people lack the social networks and informal support needed to see them through the crisis.

Employment pressures

The transition from mass industrial society to mass consumption society has been accompanied by a radical shift in social relationships within the workplace. Whereas industrial society is characterised by shared similar lifestyles and living and working conditions, consumer society is characterised by individuality in work, rest and play.

Industrial society was characterised by mass solidarity. The big industrial trades unions and employers collectives of the 1920s and 1930s are largely irrelevant today.

Consumer society is characterised by fragmentation and competition between individuals. It is this competition that has led to and allowed pathological workplace problems such as:

- Bullying
- Poor management

- o Unrealistic workloads
- o Excessive hours
- o People working above their levels of competence.

People often feel obliged to tolerate such circumstances because of their high levels of borrowing to perpetuate lifestyles at the very limit of affordability. To lose one's job is to lose one's lifestyle. To lose one's lifestyle is to lose everything that gives meaning to modern life.

In the public services such as medicine and education, the combination of extreme costs of living, excessive pressure and low incomes mean that some areas of the UK are now at risk of failing services. However, the state seems unable to comprehend the stress issue, and can only offer the old, industrial society solution of more money – either direct salary increases or housing grants – to try to retain essential staff. Meanwhile, the rate of mental illness in public services like medicine and teaching is higher than the private sector, and suicide rates in the medical profession remain the highest of all professions; and they continue to rise.

The rise of social isolation

Few young people today understand mother-in-law jokes. This is because of the massive growth in home ownership since the 1970s. In the 1930s and through to the early 1970s, it was common for newly married couples to live with the bride's family until they could find a place of their own. Even then, it was common to move to a house or flat within the same neighbourhood – hence the tension between mother-in-law/son-in-law so often diffused through humour.

These days, the expectation is that couples will find a place of their own prior to marriage. Indeed, it is common for people to want to move out of their family homes irrespective of whether they intend to marry or not.

These changes are related to structural change within the economy. As late as the 1930s, most people lived and worked within a single village or district – a process common since the industrial revolution. As the economy came out of recession in the late 1930s new industries developed in new areas. Young workers began to move in search of work. This trend continued in the post war boom, so that by the late 1970s it was common for couples to live away from their parents.

The 1980s saw further isolation with the deregulation of financial institutions allowing more mortgage borrowing and the growth of long distance commuting. It has become quite common for people to live two hours' and more travelling time from their work – allowing people to obtain higher paid employment than that available in the place where they live. In this way, work, family and home have come to be located separately for many people.

While this may have considerable economic advantages, it has social repercussions. The loss of family and neighbourhood support networks leaves people vulnerable, and is implicated in a whole range of social and psychological ills such as crime and educational failure as well as suicide.

Quality of life
One cannot, of course, rule out employment, housing, living standards and a degree of consumption of luxury items unknown to any previous generation when looking at quality of life. However, the general sense of dissatisfaction and the unprecedented levels of depression that have accompanied these trappings of modern life suggest that they are not sufficient to produce quality of life.

When considering quality of life, one must first examine what gives meaning to life. The things that give most meaning to life are stable intimate relationships and wider social networks:

"Where a family is itself isolated from wider social networks, and where formal support from the state is becoming increasingly difficult to obtain, the internal conflicts within families can come to outweigh any support they offer… It would therefore be misguided to rely on the family as the main source of support and guarantor of quality of life in future. (Watkins and Pearson 1996, p65)

In chasing home ownership, faster cars, more expensive furniture, etc, our society has lost the balance with maintaining stable intimate relationships and wider social networks. Our high and increasing rates of depression reflect this imbalance. It is an imbalance that will need to be rectified if we are to reduce our high rates of suicide.

Toxic lifestyles

Modern individuals are under more stress than ever before. The dream of a property owning democracy is turning into a nightmare in which many people do not have the income to get on the home owning ladder, but where council house sales and insufficient affordable housing leaves them paying private rents barely lower than monthly mortgage repayments. Meanwhile, social housing is in such short supply that only those from priority groups such as disabled people can look forward to relatively low rents; and only then after a long wait. Those fortunate enough to get onto the home owning ladder can often only do so at the expense of long, stressful hours at work and the loss of social life that this entails.

At the same time, in the most deprived areas of modern Britain, whole housing estates can be purchased for the cost of a single London semi, meaning that those people who might want to "get on their bikes" are trapped in un-saleable and unwanted housing.

The UK has more people working longer hours than any other EU state, even though all of the evidence suggests that long hours result in a decline in productivity in addition to causing worker burn-out. In spite of recognising tiredness as a major road traffic offence, Government has yet to limit the hours of professions such as doctors, air traffic controllers and train drivers, whose mistakes might lead to considerable loss of life.

Relative social isolation – partly the result of the privatisation of family life[8], and partly the result of working excessive hours – has left individuals more vulnerable to mental health problems than ever

---

[8] The General Household Survey 2002 shows a considerable decline in neighbourliness, suggesting that wider social networks are breaking down even among people who share close living spaces.

before. Emotionally intimate partnerships break down as soon as both partners are over-stressed for a prolonged period.

The UK divorce rate is the second highest in the EU. In 1999 there was one divorce for every two marriages. Fifty percent of second marriages end in divorce (*Social Trends 32*). Although there has been a slight fall in the rate of divorce in recent years, this is due to less people marrying rather than to divorce becoming a less necessary option.

The last two decades have seen a massive rise in home-based activities and ownership of home-based entertainment technology. The one exception to this trend has been a significant rise in cinema attendance (*Social Trends 32*). However, although not home-based, this remains a family activity that does not necessarily include wider social contact.

Thus, while experiencing more of the life stressors that endanger mental health, we are losing the social and extended family structures that have served to protect mental health through the ages. In an age of mass communication where self-esteem is measured through reference to lifestyle consumption, it is hardly a surprise that more than 10 percent of the population experience depression and/or major anxiety at any one time, or that 20 to 25 percent of the population will experience depression at some point in their lives.

In their own way, our psycho-toxic lifestyles should be as much a matter of public concern as any disease epidemic, since they seriously undermine the functioning of the NHS, particularly primary care services.

Tough on the causes of mental illness?

Too many people in the UK are living life on the edge of their ability to manage their stress. Providing things stay as they are, they can just about manage. The problem is that since the early 1970s, we have developed a society where nothing stays as it is.

The days when people could get "jobs for life" in traditional industries are long gone. With their disappearance, we have seen the end of localised family networks and the move to the privatisation of family life. Stress levels are higher than ever, but the mechanisms for de-stressing are less available.

When life-shaking events occur, the whole edifice comes tumbling down. Bereavement, redundancy, prolonged illness, separation and divorce, housing problems and debt are all common problems in everyday life. They are also factors intimately bound up with mental illness and suicide. In this sense, our focus on individuals is a form of "blaming the victim".

Those who attempt suicide are often victims of living (or attempting to live) the very stressful lifestyles our culture encourages. They become re-victimised by a system that (fails to) pick up the pieces after a suicide attempt.

Arming individuals

This report is not an attempt to call for a return to some utopian industrial society where everyone was equal and we all looked after each other – such a place never existed. The only reason people could leave their doors open in the 1950s was because they had nothing worth stealing! At the same time child abuse, violence and homicide were much more widespread than they are today.

There is much to be valued in modern life. But we must recognise new threats and dangers. Insofar as we live potentially toxic lifestyles, we need to do much more to equip individuals to deal with the consequences. Over the last two decades, successive governments have invested heavily in literacy. However, we remain emotionally illiterate.

People often do not understand their emotions. Few can put what they are feeling into words. We have difficulty finding appropriate ways of releasing pent up stresses. The classic result – one seen on a monthly basis in most newspapers – is the person who commits suicide "out of the blue". Nobody realised there was a problem. He (and it is usually he) apparently had everything to live for; a good career, nice house, nice wife, nice family. What he also had was an overload of stress that nobody had ever taught him how to deal with. In the end, he dealt with it in the only way he could see.

Those of us now in middle age – the baby boomers – may forgive our parents for not teaching us how to deal with life's stresses. The world that we were born into was stable. People lived and died in the same communities; surrounded by the same friends and family. It was only from the mid-1970s that things started to change.

Today's young adults and children have every right to blame their parents' generation for not teaching them to be emotionally literate. Ours is a world of constant change and uncertainty. It is a world where you have to be "media savvy" to understand the culture. It is a world where you have to manage your stress and your emotions if you're going to survive. The problem is that being in touch with your emotions isn't sexy; it isn't macho.

If we are going to live in a high stress, global economy and a high stress, global culture, then we need to equip all of our citizens to deal with the consequences. Government should look on it as a sort of mental health immunisation programme designed to cut down on the current epidemic of mental illness and the accompanying high rate of suicide.

Employers will need to play a role in emotional literacy and stress management. Indeed, many enlightened employers are already bringing in stress management experts to teach their core staff to manage their stress appropriately. The incentive for employers has been the realisation that it is costly to burn-out highly trained core staff; especially as low unemployment in this market segment makes replacement expensive.

Schools and colleges also need to play a part in promoting emotional literacy. This means recognising that equipping children for life in the modern world is about more than teaching them to read, write and add up. If necessary, emotional literacy should become an element of the National Curriculum, although peer mentoring programmes provide a less stressful and more credible approach.

Health promotion and health services

In addition to promoting emotional literacy, we need to do much more to promote general health. For too long, too many people (including doctors) have taken a mechanistic view of health, seeing the human body as a machine that a doctor can fix in the same way as a mechanic fixes a car. The patient is assumed to be a passive spectator, playing no part in the process of treatment, and having little responsibility for his or her own health.

This approach was based on the view that the NHS was largely an emergency treatment service, picking up the pieces when things go wrong. This approach to mental illness (and, indeed, physical illnesses) is proving highly costly both in terms of the resources used and in terms of wasted lives.

It is all too obvious in mental illness that the longer you wait before intervening, the more resources you will need, and the longer and more traumatic the recovery process. Furthermore, mental health services are wholly ineffective where the patient is the passive recipient of services. In such cases, medicines and electric shocks can be used to stabilise the patient's condition, but the patient seldom gets back to full health. Furthermore, discrimination by wider society can make full recovery or, indeed, personal growth all but impossible.

In the area of mental illness, therapies (such as cognitive behavioural therapy) that require co-operation between patient and therapist, coupled to engaged self-management and peer-to-peer support are the most effective approaches. Furthermore, the earlier the intervention, the less likely the illness will develop to become severe and enduring.

As people affected by mental illness have discovered, they are intimately involved in their own recovery. Indeed, the development of self-help and self-management approaches by patients' groups in mental health shows a growing awareness of the need to take responsibility for one's own mental health. Nor is this movement restricted to those who have, or who have had, mental illness. Those coming to terms with enduring illness such as arthritis and multiple sclerosis are also taking self-management and health promotion seriously.

We need to work toward an NHS that plays its part in the promotion of good health. This will not be easy to achieve because of the enormous resources needed to deal with today's emergencies. Nevertheless, if we do not turn things around, we will never be able to afford the NHS that we want. This means that the NHS has to find ways of releasing resources to intervene in those cases where early intervention will result in considerable savings later on by preventing a moderate condition becoming a severe and enduring one. In the case of depression, for example, few people can secure treatment other than antidepressant drugs while their depression is considered mild to moderate. However, few people actually recover just by taking antidepressants. Rather, antidepressants work to stabilise patients' conditions so that other therapies can work. In other words, much of the money that goes on antidepressants every year is wasted because the other support and services required to promote full recovery are absent – the patient's condition may have temporarily improved, but only at the cost of a relapse later on.

There is an added incentive to free resources for early interventions. The CBI (December 2001) has found that 60 percent of people who are off work with illness for more than 6 weeks lose their jobs. This means that our current management of health is a burden in terms of lost production, lost tax revenue and increased spending on benefits. Where early intervention can return someone to work, it makes economic sense to act.

State interventions

Encouraging individuals to take responsibility for their own health is, in and of itself, an important need – particularly as the process of globalisation is accelerating the rate of change and uncertainty. Developing health services that engage in health promotion and early intervention where this can make a difference, is also an important element in reversing the mental illness epidemic and the high suicide rate. However, the state must play a part by using its power to plan and legislate in order to curb some of the more excessive stressors in modern Britain.

The two key areas where the state can play a role are in setting the framework for employment, and in the planning of our infrastructure.

Much of the legislation governing practices in the workplace is derived from EU directives aimed at preventing unfair competition. Thus, health and safety law prevents an employer undercutting competitors by failing to take measures to protect the health and safety of employees.

UK health and safety law already protects the mental health of employees. However, successive governments have tended to be weaker on enforcement in this area than is the case for physical health and safety. Furthermore, the UK government has negotiated a number of opt-outs that allow employers to escape their responsibilities, perhaps the most important of these being the opt-out on restricting working hours. This allows workers to choose to work more than the proposed maximum of 48 hours per week[9]. This is despite of masses of evidence showing that longer hours cause productivity to fall, and seriously impair the health of those working them. To give one example, the medical profession is exempted from the regulations governing working hours. It also has the highest rates of stress related illness and the highest suicide rate of all professions in the UK.

Government must take workplace stress seriously. This means tightening up those areas where previous governments opted out of health and safety regulation. It means encouraging the courts to hand out exemplary damages against firms guilty of injuring the mental health of employees. It also means increasing the criminal sanctions available against firms and individual managers who abuse and/or bully employees. Such an approach would allow good employers to benefit from the removal of unfair competition from those who injure health in order to try to gain a short-term competitive edge.

---

[9] The degree to which a "choice" may be the result of coercion by an employer and/or the result of employees reliance on overtime to meet debts isn't taken into account in this opt-out.

Government will also need to tackle the way we live currently. We cannot go on with the current shortage of housing that has caused commuting to be a daily experience for too many people. Instead of using time away from work to manage stress, too many people spend it getting more stressed on our overloaded transport network.

In some areas of the country, individuals are beginning to walk with their feet, accepting lower paid employment close to home. Some employers cannot provide high enough salaries to encourage people to commute or to enable them to buy houses near their work. This is something government will find increasingly hard to ignore. However, when looking to the future, government will need to think in terms of enabling people to live balanced lives – work, rest and play, not work, rest and commute!

By tackling the wider, unnecessary causes of stress within the UK, we can begin to lower the numbers of people who develop stress related illness. Furthermore, by investing in emotional literacy, we can arm individuals to deal appropriately with the inevitable stress of modern living. By creating an NHS that promotes health and acts to prevent low-level conditions becoming emergencies, we save people with problems becoming disabled and seriously ill. This approach can lower the rate of mental illness, and result in a corresponding fall in the suicide rate. Furthermore, in the long term it will free up NHS resources for those with the most severe and enduring illnesses.

Alternatively, we can continue with a policy that is overloading the NHS, and creating mental illness and suicide epidemics. In the end it is a political choice.

Conclusion

In spite of decades of suicide reduction initiatives, the UK suicide rate remains stubbornly high. Indeed, suicide is now a bigger cause of death than road traffic accidents, and is the single biggest killer of young people.

In most cases of suicide and attempted suicide, the individual will have been affected by depression prior to their attempt. It is no accident that the precipitating causes of suicide correspond to the causes of depression:

- Bereavement
- Redundancy
- Debt
- Housing problems
- Separation/divorce/relationship problems
- Prolonged illness
- Overwork.

Those taking part in the survey simply confirmed the importance of these factors in precipitating suicide attempts. Their comments about how they felt often serve to show how the psychological pain and distorted thinking that is a part of all depression can make suicide seem rational. For example, those who felt that their families would be better off without them now realise how much their families would have missed them.

Interestingly, almost all of the factors that precipitate suicide attempts are socio-economic rather than psychiatric problems. This is especially important if these precipitating factors are on-going while psychiatric treatment is being attempted.

Psychiatric and psychological approaches have proved effective in tackling many of the factors that predispose people to depression and suicide:

- o Low self-esteem
- o Perfectionism
- o Passivity
- o Sense of isolation
- o Feelings of helplessness and hopelessness
- o Guilt.

However, it is almost impossible to work on these issues if the socio-economic precipitating factors are on-going. One wonders whether employment tribunals, divorce lawyers or debt management specialists ought not be the first professionals to treat most people with mental illness, leaving the psychiatrist for later on. Certainly we need more flexibility in service provision to make sure that those with mental health problems have access to the full range of services at an early stage.

Many professionals working within mental health are coming around to the benefits of a holistic approach that puts patients at the centre of their treatment. For example, instead of dismissing the benefits of housing support or debt advice because these aren't "medical services", many within mental health see that until someone's housing or debt situation is sorted out, their mental health is unlikely to improve.

Unfortunately, all too often both mental illness and suicide continue to be treated as solely medical conditions with a focus on treating individual pathology. In the case of those deemed to be at risk of harming themselves, this has meant calls for more supervision, more detention, more medicating of individuals, either to remove them from the means of harm or to remove the means of harm from them. Whether this is conducive to eventual recovery or how this impacts on the mental health of the wider population goes unasked.

The evidence suggests that these practices do little to lower suicide rates but a great deal to deter those at risk from seeking help.

Our focus on individuals also fails because we lack the ability to accurately predict suicidal behaviour. Many successful suicides are by people deemed to have been at no-risk or low-risk to themselves by mental health professionals. On the other side of the coin, as the survey shows, many suicidal people are ignored by overloaded NHS mental health services. There is more than a suspicion that we are detaining many people who are not at risk, while discharging or ignoring the needs of many who are!

It is the focus on individual pathology that is at fault. Some benefits have been achieved by measures to reduce the availability of the means of suicide, for example, curbs on paracetamol sales, the change to natural gas and the introduction of catalytic converters. A move away from prescribing older, toxic antidepressants would be the next logical step in this type of approach to suicide reduction. However, these measures have not brought about large falls in the overall rate of suicide, suggesting that their main long-term effect is to displace suicidal behaviour to other methods.

If governments are serious about reducing the rate of suicide, they need to understand that the rate of suicide is, itself, an indicator of the wellbeing of the whole society. By this measure, the UK has been getting progressively sicker since the mid-1970s.

The real choice facing governments concerned with reducing the suicide rate is whether they are prepared to make early interventions to prevent suicidal behaviour ever arising, or whether they are content simply to pick up the pieces after suicide has occurred.

Our current approach of targeting individuals fails because proper identification of risk is impossible. Furthermore, our health services are too over-stretched to operate in a preventative manner. Introducing more detention and compulsion into the mental health system will simply serve to deter those who may become suicidal without treatment from coming forward, while adding to the workload of overstretched health professionals.

We need to free up resources to prevent and mitigate mental health problems before they become so serious as to make suicide appear a reasonable option. An important part of this approach will be making resources available to provide effective early interventions using a package of medical, psychological, social and economic services to prevent people with problems becoming ill, and to quickly rehabilitate those with relatively mild needs.

We also need a genuine effort to promote mental health. To achieve this, while continuing to provide services to people affected by mental illness, will require a three-fold approach aimed at:

> Promoting emotional literacy through education and through young people's peer mentoring schemes
> Releasing resources for mental health promotion and preventative health services
> Using regulation and legislation to do away with the worst stress-creating practices in our society.

None of these measures are easy to achieve. None are without cost. Furthermore, the results will take time to filter through. In the end, these are hard political choices for which there may be little in the way of short-term electoral pay-offs.

Our political leaders may continue to focus on individual pathology and on locking people up, with the result that we will meet World Health Organisation predictions that mental illness will become the second biggest cause of ill health in the UK by 2020 – with the implication that the suicide rate will increase at least proportionately.

Alternatively, we can start to address the wider social, economic and educational factors that underlie mental illness and suicide. To paraphrase Mr Blair, to be tough on suicide, we need to be tough on *all* of the causes of suicide.

Further reading

BBC News Online, *'Suicide genes' identified.* 6th April 2001.

Burns, David D. MD., 1990. *The Feeling Good Handbook.* Plume. New York

Brock, A., Baker, A., Griffiths, C., Jackson, G., Fegan, G. and Marshall, D. 2006. 'Suicide trends and geographical variations in the United Kingdom, 1991-2004'. In *Health Statistics Quarterly 31.* Office for National Statistics, Autumn 2006.

Calder, A., 1992. *The People's War: Britain 1939-1945.* Pimlico. London.

CBI. December 2001. *Business and healthcare for the 21st Century.* CBI. London.

Department of Health, 2001. *Safety First: Five-year report of the National Confidential Inquiry into Suicide and Homicide by People with Mental Illness.* Department of Health Publications. London.

Department of Health, 2002. *Making it Happen: A guide to delivering mental health promotion.* Department of Health Publications. London.

Donnellan, C., (ed) 2000. *Issues Volume 51: Self-harm and Suicide.* Independence Educational Publishers. Cambridge.

Durkheim, E., 1888. *Suicide: A study in sociology.* Routledge and Keegan Paul. London.

Gunnell, D. and Frankel, S., 1994. *Prevention of Suicide: aspirations and evidence* British Medical Journal, May 1994; 308: 1227-1233.

Hegarty, James D. 1995. *Suicidal And Violent Behaviour Associated With The Use Of Fluoxetine .*

Hobsawm, E., 1968. *Industry and Empire*. Penguin Books. Middlesex.

Independent on Sunday – various articles in the Mental Health Campaign series 2002.

National Assembly for Wales., 1999. *Welsh Health Survey 1998*. Government Statistical Service. Norwich.

Pritchard, C., 1995. *Suicide – The Ultimate Rejection: A psycho-social study*. Open University Press. Philadelphia

Samaritans, 2000. *Youth Matters 2000 – A cry for help*.

Shaw, M., Dorling, D. and Davey Smith, G., 2002. *Mortality and Political Climate: How suicide rates have risen during periods of Conservative government, 1901-2000*. Journal of Epidemiology and Community Health 2002; 56: 723-725.

Watkins, T. and Pearson, N., 1996. *Residential Homes: Quality of Life and Quality of Service*. Welsh Consumer Council. Cardiff.

Wilkinson, R.G. 1996. *Unhealthy Societies: The afflictions of inequality* London. Routledge.

Williams, M., 1997. *Suicide and Attempted Suicide*. Penguin books. London.

Wright, C., 2001. (unpublished) *Depression and Suicide: A training package prepared for the South Wales Police Force*.

About Life Surfing

Life Surfing is a Cardiff-based not-for-profit Community Interest Company that was established to provide a coaching, mentoring and training approach for people experiencing common life problems that can cause stress, anxiety and depression.

Our mission is to help people learn to cope with life without the need to call on over-stretched NHS services that are better deployed to help people with severe mental illness.

Over the years we have found that there is a huge amount that people can do to develop their personal resources and to foster their own wellbeing. In most cases, the real need is for encouragement, support, knowledge and skills.

This is what Life Surfing offers.

We have developed a range of services – one-to-one wellbeing coaching, training workshops, mentoring groups and a range of publications - to give you the knowledge, skills and motivation needed to address life's issues and overcome stress-related problems in a healthy way, and to promote your long-term personal wellbeing.

For further information, please visit the Life Surfing website:

www. life-surfing.com

info@life-surfing.com

Or you can contact us on: 0300 321 4514 / 07922 537 646

Life Surfing, Box 124, R&R Consulting Centre
41 St. Isan Road
Heath
Cardiff CF14 4LW